QUOTATIONS
FROM
PREMIER
CHOU EN-LAI

QUOTATIONS FROM PREMIER CHOU EN-LAI

A COLLINS ASSOCIATES BOOK

Thomas Y. Crowell Company
New York · Established 1834

Copyright © 1973 by Collins Associates

All rights reserved. Except for use in a review, the reproduction or utilization of this work in any form or by any electronic, mechanical, or other means, now known or hereafter invented, including xerography, photocopying, and recording, and in any information storage and retrieval system is forbidden without the written permission of the publisher. Published simultaneously in Canada by Fitzhenry & Whiteside Limited, Toronto.

Designed by Jacqueline Thibodeau

Manufactured in the United States of America

ISBN 0-690-66418-4

1 2 3 4 5 6 7 8 9 10

Library of Congress Cataloging in Publication Data

Chou, Ên-lai, 1898-
Quotations from Premier Chou En-lai.

"A Collins Associates book."
 Bibliography: p.
 I. Title.
DS778.C593A57   951.04   72-14181
ISBN 0-690-66418-4

CONTENTS

INTRODUCTION

Of the many political leaders in the world today only a few can be called statesmen. It is the rare politician who has the experience, the understanding of foreign countries, the long-term historical perspective, and the grasp of the subtleties of international power that elevate him to the rank of world statesman. Chou En-lai, the Premier of the People's Republic of China, is one of those few.

Chou En-lai has been an international figure for almost fifty years. Before 1949, when the Communists grew from a small band of struggling guerrilla fighters into the major force in the Chinese Revolution, Chou was their representative in dealings with other factions and other countries. And since the 1949 liberation, Chou has been the foremost foreign policy maker and spokesman for the most populous nation in the world. He has not only molded Chinese foreign policy; he has also played the important role of international interpreter: he explains China to the rest of the world and interprets foreign developments for his people. Wherever and whenever there is a juncture between China and another part of the world, Chou En-lai is there trying to develop mutual understanding.

On the Chinese domestic scene, his power has been remarkably stable during the twenty-three years since liberation, and today he is second only to Chairman Mao Tse-tung in the leadership hierarchy. But it is his stature as international statesman and his role as interpreter-mediator between China and the rest of the world that is most important to us in the West.

This collection is an attempt to understand Chou En-lai's role as international "middleman." Through Chou's own words we discover how he explains China to the West and how he views the United States and the rest of the world. We have drawn mainly on Chou's conversations with foreigners rather than from his domestic speeches and writings in order to focus on Chou the international statesman.

Chou the man—his wit, his style, his personality—was another reason for excerpting more of Chou's conversations in relatively informal settings in contrast to his more formal policy pronouncements. The Premier obviously enjoys his long, unstructured talks with visitors, and from these relaxed encounters a vivid sense of his personality emerges.

A number of Americans have had the opportunity to speak to Chou recently and have been impressed with both his physical and intellectual capacities. James Reston of *The New York Times* commented after meeting Chou, "He has the coolest eye and most penetrating way of looking at you of any man I think I've ever seen." His expressive eyes are framed by wonderful heavy peaked eyebrows ("John L. Lewis eyebrows" as Reston described them). He dresses in a simple gray tunic and trousers, but often takes off his jacket and chats with guests in his shirt sleeves. As one observer noted, the main impression is of a mind of tremendous acuity.

As a handsome youth, Chou was an amateur actor, often taking the female role because traditional Chinese drama did not customarily permit women to appear on stage. He obviously has not lost his flair for the dramatic. An exceptionally observant traveler, Australian journalist-scholar Ross Terrill, noticed how Chou's "small, fine hands, moving sinuously as if direct from the shoulder, serve his rapidly varying tone and mood." He watched Chou's hands "fly like an actor's in the air" when he attacked former Japanese Prime Minister Sato. The actor's grace serves the diplomat well. The Premier is, as André Malraux has observed, "obviously an intellectual." Yet his urbane sophistication and intellectual gentility do not seem to alienate him from the overwhelmingly working-class Chinese population. According to all reports, this grandson of a distinguished Ch'ing Dynasty mandarin is extraordinarily popular not only with citizens of the People's Republic but among Chinese communities in other parts of the world as well.

His energy is incredible. He often talks with evening visitors until breakfast time. He has impressed American visitors with his sharpness—remembering both their English and their given Chinese names, knowing the details of their trip itineraries, and displaying what Harrison Salisbury of *The New York Times* described as his "encyclopedic" knowledge of the United States.

Chou plays two special "games" with foreign guests: he amazes and flatters them by speaking at least a few words of their language and by casually dropping facts about their country. For example, when Nobel-laureate George Wald met with Chou, the Premier surprised the scientist by mentioning that both Wald and Henry Kissinger were Harvard University faculty members. He regularly reads American news reports—including full transcripts of Presidential news conferences—and is well-versed about even the minor issues and personalities in American politics.

Chou discusses foreign developments both to impress visitors with his own storehouse of knowledge and to add to it. As journalist Seymour Topping noted, he bombards foreign guests with questions about every aspect of life in their countries. He has an insatiable curiosity. While on one level he simply seems to be enjoying the rambling conversation and joking, on another level he is making the most of the opportunity. There are nuances of foreign life that he learns best by talking with visitors, so he unobtrusively maneuvers the discussion in these directions. Back in 1937, author Edgar Snow observed that Chou is "a person of charm and urbanity in control of a tough, supple and highly disciplined brain."

Chou is modest in regard both to himself and to China's achievements. He has been heard frequently berating himself for his blundering at the Geneva Conference in 1954. And he often warns foreigners not to be uncritically enthusiastic about the progress China has made since 1949. Once, emphasizing that there were still many backward aspects to Chinese life, he suggested that he himself might have some old-fashioned, non-revolutionary ideas. When one American recently sought to flatter China by disparaging the United

States, Chou responded: "Thank you for your kind words but I don't think we have done so well. Do you really think that? I don't quite believe that." And as Harrison Salisbury noted after meeting Chou:

> He likes to maintain a coldly realistic attitude toward China's policies and repeatedly goes out of his way to note that China has made many mistakes and that she is by no means as perfect as some of her friends like to say.

Everyone who meets him finds him looking and acting younger than his years, yet Chou seems acutely conscious of his aging. He often refers to his age. He told Salisbury that at his "advanced age" he cannot look forward to visiting the United States, and he is preoccupied with issues of age and youth. Chou told James Reston that he and his colleagues grew old in the long revolutionary struggle and didn't come to power until they were already in their fifties; therefore, he said, he thought a lot about problems of succession and tried to encourage younger leaders.

Premier Chou En-lai is the link between China and the world. Beyond his physical and intellectual abilities, Chou has an even more important qualification for playing this mediator role: his rich experience in dealing with foreigners. Chou is one of the few Chinese leaders who has traveled extensively abroad and who has had almost constant contact with foreign representatives. He studied and worked in France as a young man in the 1920's. Even before the Communists came to power in 1949, he served as negotiator with both the Kuomintang and the foreign powers. When General George Marshall tried to bring peace between the Kuomintang and the Communists, he held months of discussions with Chou En-lai and came to respect him as the ablest negotiator he had ever encountered.

After 1949, Chou made frequent trips to Europe, Asia, Africa, and the Soviet Union. We in the West heard most about his highly publicized activities at the Geneva Conference in 1954 and the Third-World Bandung Conference of 1955 and during his tour of Africa in 1964.

The years between 1949 and 1971 must have been difficult for Chou as a statesman. The cold war, non-recognition by the United States (and by many American allies), and China's own weakness after a debilitating civil war limited her international options. While China did make friends among the developing nations of the Third World, many other nations were not open to trade with China. Even during those frustrating years, Chou was trying to reach out to other countries. When he tried to establish normal diplomatic contact, however, he was often spurned. The most poignant instance occurred at Geneva in 1954. John Foster Dulles returned to the conference room one day after lunch and found only Chou En-lai there. Chou held out his hand; Dulles refused to shake it. The American Secretary of State then turned and left the room. Now even an American President has toasted the Premier in Peking, and China has regained her seat in the United Nations—and Chou recalls the Dulles insult with a feeling of triumph over tremendous odds.

When we collected Chou's statements on Chinese policy toward the United States, we found a remarkable consistency over the years. Even in the bitter cold war atmosphere of the 1950's, he expressed hopes for Chinese-American friendship. He always remained firm on the Taiwan issue—demanding that the United States desist from interfering in a problem internal to China and withdraw its forces from Taiwan and the Taiwan Strait—but he also constantly stressed that the Chinese people wanted to be friends with the American people.

Chou's attempts to end China's isolation and his campaign against foreign intervention were based on his belief that international relations founded on equality were in his country's interest. Chou is often described as the pragmatist, the practical politician, in contrast to Mao Tse-tung who is portrayed as the ideologue, the political visionary. But this characterization of Chou is false if drawn too crudely. Chou En-lai is unusually sensitive to the practical realities of both China and the world, but he also is a loyal Communist. He was a revolutionary leader in the Long March; indeed, his entire life has been committed to building a socialist China. His words naturally reflect both a realistic understanding of actual situations and his own political values.

Premier Chou's long struggle to gain for China the international position he felt she deserved has finally produced results. His efforts to break down the hostile isolation of China have succeeded, and the changed world situation is more positive not just for the Chinese but for all of us. Simultaneously, Chou himself is gaining international respect, a far cry from the cold war days when he was treated as an international outlaw. Chou has little time for savoring accolades; his responsibilities are heavier than ever. Ties with the United States are still in the condition of fragile newness, and relations with other powers—especially the Soviet Union and Japan—are equally delicate. Chou's skills as negotiator and statesman are needed now as never before.

There are pressing demands on his time and energy at home in China as well. He has always been a respected leader on the domestic scene, but his astute handling of the conflicts of the Cultural Revolution, along with the decline of other leaders, have put him at the apex of power today. Chou's personal magnetism and negotiating skill made him one of the few Chinese leaders who could relate to the young Red Guards. On one remarkable occasion he was confronted by a mob of overzealous Red Guards who were ready to do violence to everyone and everything, including Chou himself. He talked with the youths all night, calmed them, and persuaded them that non-violent criticism was more effective and more revolutionary than violence. The Premier made himself indispensable by his active and wise leadership in restoring order after the Cultural Revolution.

Thus the aging Premier is more influential today, more respected, and more needed than ever before. The changed world situation opens up new opportunities for him to act as a truly international statesman and to indulge his personal fascination with the West. For example, no one who has met Chou doubts that he would love to visit the United States— a trip to the United Nations in New York would be both a personal adventure and political triumph for him.

Yet because of his age and the demands of domestic Chinese politics, Chou may never be able to travel to the United States. It is our hope that this collection of Chou's words will give the western reader an understanding of how he would want to interpret the Chinese experience to us and how he sees us and the rest of the world. But most of all, readers will have a vicarious encounter with Chou the man.

The Editors

NOTE: Although Chou En-lai is quite relaxed in his discussions with foreign guests and often urges them to tape-record the entire conversation, he sometimes remembers to warn of possible inaccuracies. As he said when he met with a group from the Committee of Concerned Asian Scholars:

> And if any of you have taken any tape recorders with you, you can also record the talk here if you want. Since we are meeting you, of course we will speak freely. Maybe I will say something wrong here, or perhaps . . . the interpreter might interpret wrong. It doesn't matter. It's a free exchange of views.

I.

CHOU–THE MAN

A FREE EXCHANGE OF VIEWS

"No, none of us have kept a diary—not Mao or Lin Piao or I, and none of us want to write our memoirs." Maybe, though, he continued, a history of China from the Opium War on should be prepared, and perhaps it would be a good idea to try to get the record down on tape, but, he added, "we are not quite accustomed to the tape recorder in China yet."

> James Reston, "Transcript of Interview with Chou," August 5, 1971; *The New York Times, Report from Red China,* New York, Avon Books, 1971

And if any of you have taken any tape recorders with you, you can also record the talk here if you want. Since we are meeting you, of course we will speak freely. Maybe I will say something wrong here, or perhaps these other two comrades might say something wrong, or the interpreter might interpret wrong. It doesn't matter. It's a free exchange of views. People should be allowed to say wrong things, isn't that so? Otherwise what is the need for exchange? If everyone had the same view, what would be the purpose of an exchange of views? And how would we be able to act about these ideas?

> Interview, Committee of Concerned Asian Scholars Friendship Delegation to China, July 19, 1971

ON HIS FREQUENT MEETINGS WITH VISITING AMERICANS

Since last April one more item has been added to my work, to receive American friends. The atmosphere of our conversations has taken us back to the old days in northern Shensi,

Wuhan, Chungking, and Nanking, and makes us feel relaxed. You'd better not look upon me as the Premier but rather as an ordinary Chinese. As the Premier, I will feel more restrained when I talk. If you take down everything I say, I won't feel so free. Then I'd have to follow Dr. Kissinger's example, and say that this is an off-the-record briefing. I am not used to a briefing conference; I have not yet learned to do it.

Interview, with John McCook Roots, Thomas Manton, George Wald, et al., January 31, 1972

We fully agree with your opinion that you should go among the masses. There is not much to talk about with us (*laughter*) —just the same old issues. And once you read the newspapers you will see that what Mr. Chou En-lai says has all been printed in the newspapers (*laughter*) and to listen to it is nauseating. (*Laughter.*) Isn't that so? And I support that idea of yours. For instance, you have all been taken to either factories or people's communes or schools and other people have already been to them. And when you go back you will say, "All the news about those places has already been printed in the Hong Kong newspapers—what interest is there in our reporting about the same things?" I believe it was a lady among you who expressed such feelings.

Interview, Committee of Concerned Asian Scholars Friendship Delegation to China, July 19, 1971

CHOU COMMENTS ON YOUTH AND AGE

During the Pacific War there had been a lot of opportunities for the Chinese and American people to contact each other.

And taking myself as an example, I know a lot of old friends from your country of an older generation.

Interview, Committee of Concerned Asian Scholars Friendship Delegation to China, July 19, 1971

You say that the youth are better than the older generation. We also agree. We say that those who come later become better. I am much older than they are, and I talk so much that there's bound to be a flaw, when you talk a lot. So it's not a very favorable aspect to be a premier at such an advanced age.

Interview, Committee of Concerned Asian Scholars Friendship Delegation to China, July 19, 1971

ON THE YOUTHFULNESS OF WHITE HOUSE STAFFERS WHO ACCOMPANIED NIXON TO CHINA

We have too many elderly people in our government, so on this point we should learn from you.

Newsweek, March 6, 1972

CHOU VIEWS THE REVOLUTION

Comrade Liu [Ning], we must be patient. For the sake of our revolution we must be very patient. For the sake of our revolution we can play the role of a concubine, even a prostitute, if need be . . .

1927; Liu Ning, *The Autobiography of a Proletarian*

Five years after the Chinese May 4 movement great changes had taken place, the great revolution had already begun. And you will recall that the Great Proletarian Cultural Revolution has just now gone into the fifth year. In fact today is precisely the fifth anniversary of Chairman Mao's return to Peking. You probably have seen an article on the sixteenth of July commemorating the fifth anniversary of Chairman Mao swimming the Yangtze River. But our papers forgot to republish the photo of Chairman Mao swimming the Yangtze River. They try to be creative but yet they've forgotten.

Although the time may not be so long, if one puts in effort and struggles hard, great results will take place. For instance, when the Chinese Communist party was founded in 1921 there were only twelve deputies to the First Party Congress, and the total number of Communist party members at that time did not exceed seventy. But only about three years later in 1924, it had changed tremendously. By 1926 our forces were already above fifty thousand. In 1924, Mr. Sun Yat-sen's Kuomintang started cooperation with Comrade Mao Tse-tung's CCP. Such tremendous changes took place within a period of only five years. What is more, your era is totally different from the era of those days. History will not re-enact itself, and while we can make the comparison, it will not completely reenact itself. Since we always say that times are advancing, and time will not turn back, so we hope to see you again in five years. (*Laughter and applause.*)

Interview, Committee of Concerned Asian Scholars Friendship Delegation to China, July 19, 1971

Chou En-lai, standing in dark overcoat, and Commander-in-Chief
Chu Teh, seated beside driver in a former U.S. army weapons carrier.
The man in the center, whose face is hidden by his hands, is believed
to be Mao Tse-tung. *Wide World Photos.*

ON THE NIXON TRIP TO CHINA

The inevitable in history often comes about through the accidental. The fact that the people of the United States and China wanted contacts became ripe, and Chairman Mao happened to take an interest.

> Interview, with a group of visiting Americans, including journalist John McCook Roots, *The New York Times*, February 6, 1972

ON THE LIBERATION OF WOMEN

"Are women more intelligent than men?" asked the President of the Premier on seeing women technicians in the exhibits and advertising his question as "delicate."

"In the majority of work, what men can do, women can do," said the Premier. He pointed out that one of the interpreters assigned to the Nixon party could do her job so well because her husband performs more domestic chores than his wife.

"Be sure your husband doesn't stay home and look at TV," said the President to the interpreter.

> *The New York Times*, February 28, 1972

Men and women should be equal, but there are still old habits that hinder complete equality. We must carry on the struggle. It may take ten or twenty years.

> Interview, with William Attwood, Robert L. Keatley, and Seymour Topping, July 21, 1971. *The New York Times*, July 23, 1971

CHOU: There are a lot of people who would like to go [to the U.S.]. Of course I believe that you will also welcome not only men, but also women. (*Laughter.*)

YAO WEN-YÜAN [member of Politburo]: And complete equality in numbers. I believe that the main thing should be the content.

CHOU: It also would be a good thing to make it equal in numbers. But even though we are a socialist country, a country of the dictatorship of the proletariat, yet, still, male chauvinism comes up now and then. Of course, subconsciously.

CHANG CH'UN-CH'IAO [member of Politburo]: Today, seated here among the Chinese comrades, the number of men and women are not equal yet.

CHOU: See, he's criticizing me. Yet I have tried my utmost to pay attention to the fact. I have paid relative attention to it. When I invited the comrades from Tsinghua University, I invited one man and one woman.

> Interview, Committee of Concerned Asian Scholars Friendship Delegation to China, July 19, 1971

[Referring to a top-level scientific board] It's true we still only have three women out of a board membership of twenty-one, but our quota is nine and we're gradually getting there.

> Interview, with Dr. Arthur W. Galston and Dr. Ethan Signer, spring 1971. *The New York Times,* June 5, 1971

VIEWS ON SMOKING AND DRINKING

Very few women smoke in China and as a rule young people don't smoke, so over half the country doesn't smoke.

> Interview, with a group of visiting Americans, including journalist John McCook Roots, *The New York Times*, February 6, 1972

You Americans don't smoke because you're all afraid of cancer. It's because of the propaganda that's printed on your cigarette packages. But it isn't necessarily true that smoking will shorten your life.

> The Boston *Globe*, July 5, 1972

[Jokingly, on the import market in the United States for maotai, a clear 60-proof sorghum liquor]—We will not be able to supply so much maotai.

> Interview, with William Attwood, Robert L. Keatley, and Seymour Topping, July 21, 1971. *The New York Times*, July 23, 1971

AUDREY TOPPING, PHOTOGRAPHER AND WRITER, REPORTS ON
A DINNER CHOU HAD ON JUNE 21, 1971, WITH JOURNALISTS
SEYMOUR TOPPING, ROBERT KEATLEY, AND WILLIAM ATTWOOD
AND THEIR WIVES

Mr. Chou recalled how maotai was discovered in Kweichow
Province during the Long March. He said that the water
comes from the Mao Tai River and is particularly favorable
for making liquor because it doesn't go to your head. When
this was greeted by skeptical laughter he added that he had
consumed a lot of foreign liquor and none could be compared to maotai on this point.

"You can drink three glasses tonight and I guarantee nothing
will happen," he said.

The New York Times, Report from
Red China

CHOU SPEAKS HIS MIND

[On moon shots] We have so many things to do on earth.
Why go to the moon? It is a great waste and the people must
pay for it.

Interview, with William Attwood,
Robert L. Keatley, and Seymour
Topping, July 21, 1971. The New
York Times, July 23, 1971

Such a small place as Indochina, with a small population. Yet
such a huge sum has been spent.

James Reston, "Transcript of Inter-
view with Chou," August 5, 1971;
The New York Times, Report from
Red China

AUDREY TOPPING REPORTS ON A DINNER SHE AND HER FATHER,
CANADIAN DIPLOMAT CHESTER A. RONNING, HAD WITH
CHOU ON MAY 1, 1971

The greatest pollution has taken place in the most advanced
industrial countries. Developing countries, like China, which
are not as far advanced industrially can benefit from the ex-
periences of these countries to avoid similar problems.

> *The New York Times, Report from
> Red China*

If it [abstract art] has no meaning, what value has it for the
people?

> August 30, 1960. Edgar Snow, *Red
> China Today, The Other Side of
> the River*

UPON HEARING A VISITING AMERICAN CALL KISSINGER
A "METTERNICH"

How can there crop up in the present day a Metternich of
the nineteenth century?

> Interview, with John McCook Roots,
> Thomas Manton, George Wald, et
> al., January 31, 1972

I've said that the Chinese people are friendly to the American people, the two peoples have been friendly with each

Paris-Match.

other in the past, and in the future they should all the more live together in friendship, because the Chinese people have now stood up.

That was said far back in 1955 at the Bandung conference. Afterwards, we tried to accept the visit of some American correspondents to China, but John Foster Dulles's State Department did not approve of that. And so, since the way was blocked by the U.S. Government, then we on our side would no longer want any such contacts. We have thus been cut off for more than twenty years, but it doesn't matter.

But now since there are some changes in the world, then we should see to it no damage is done to anyone, that concern should be shown to the wronged party and the wronged party should not continue to be wronged.

James Reston, "Transcript of Interview with Chou," August 5, 1971; The New York Times, Report from Red China

"I understand philosophy, but computers are too complicated for me," President Nixon said to Premier Chou during a tour of Shanghai's industrial exhibition yesterday.

"I don't understand them either, but you have to pay attention to them," said the Premier.

The New York Times, February 28, 1972

ON THE USE OF CLASSIFIED DOCUMENTS

Without question, state secrets must be kept unconditionally, and no relaxation of alertness can be tolerated. The question is to define correctly what is meant by state secrets and not to extend the limit arbitrarily, thereby causing damage to the work and difficulties to the workers.

"Report on the Question of Intellectuals," January 14, 1956

ON BRIDGING THE GENERATION GAP

Glenn Cowan, our hippie, made the mistake of addressing him as "Mr. Chairman." He asked what he thought of the hippie movement in the United States—a question that was completely unexpected and seemed to catch not only Mr. Chou off guard, but also the rest of the Americans. . . .

"Perhaps youth is dissatisfied with the present situation," he said. "Youth wants to seek the truth and out of this search various forms of change are bound to come forth. Thus, this is a kind of transitional period. Youth goes through various practices and different things. Practice is very important because theory without practice is useless. And there are different kinds of ideology."

"When we were young," he continued, "it was the same, too."

He then noted Cowan's long hair and seemed amused by it, and said that the English and Japanese youth also had long hair. He didn't actually criticize it, but we inferred that he wouldn't recommend it to his youth. . . .

"We agree that young people should try different things, but we should try to find something in common with the great majority," Mr. Chou said in what seemed a polite pitch for the world's short haired.

Interview, with members of the United States table tennis team, *The New York Times,* April 15, 1971

We have heard you have said that you think that the present youth movement in the United States is similar to the May 4 movement in China, at the present stage. I was also a participant in the May 4 movement and meeting you it seems that I have gone back fifty-four years—fifty-two years. But I don't think it's exactly the same. Perhaps you also have a bit of the Red Guard movement of China in your movement now. So you have something of both eras. Is that so? . . .

And during the May 4 movement in China we also liked to pick young women to be our leaders. There were a lot of instances like that. For instance, my wife, Comrade Deng Yingqiao, has done that work. At that time she was only fifteen. You see at that time, we had a majority of middle-school students in the movement and the college students were only a minority, and now you are all college graduates.

Therefore you have entered the Red Guard period. We will have to ask these two comrades to tell you something about the Red Guard movement. The Red Guards called themselves members of the "service committee," or members of the "general service committee." It is also a Red Guard trend of thought that they don't like to be called "minister" or "section head" or "director." They like to think that's all bureaucratic and therefore we must do away with the bureaucratic structure and call ourselves "service personnel" of the people. And I think that you also have the same idea. We also see that now some of the men wear their hair long and also grow beards to express their dissatisfaction with the present state of affairs. There are two men here with large beards. There are not many with long hair. . . .

During the May 4 movement there was a situation which was opposite to your present situation. That is, there were girls who shaved their heads. During the May 4 movement there was also a girl who took part in the movement who was from the Hui nationality. Her name was Guo Dongzhen. She sacrificed her life during the civil war period of 1927–37 and she at that time shaved her head clean—during the May 4 movement—to express dissatisfaction. During the Red Guard movement there was a different trend. At that time they liked to wear coarse clothes, army uniforms, and arm-bands, and also clothes that were patched that had as many patches as possible.

Interview, Committee of Concerned Asian Scholars Friendship Delegation to China, July 19, 1971

Your criticism hit the right spot. (*Laughter.*) So we welcome very much this spiritual help from you. It is "rectifying wrong ideas." That is Chairman Mao's wording. It is not brainwashing, it is rectifying erroneous ideas. I haven't thought of a way to wash one's brain yet. In a certain way I would also like to have my brain washed because I also have old ideas in my mind. I have already passed seventy-three; how can it be said that I have no old ideas in my head, because I came over from the old society?

Interview, Committee of Concerned Asian Scholars Friendship Delegation to China, July 19, 1971

AUDREY TOPPING REPORTS ON A DINNER SHE AND HER FATHER, CANADIAN DIPLOMAT CHESTER A. RONNING, HAD WITH CHOU ON MAY 1, 1971

The Premier, wearing a gray tunic suit and smoking a Central Flowery Kingdom cigarette, was in a jovial mood and looked much younger than his seventy-three years. He asked why Mr. Ronning had retired "so early."

"I did not retire early," Mr. Ronning replied. "I remained in the foreign service until I was seventy-one. Canadians are supposed to retire at sixty-five."

The Premier smiled broadly and replied: "Well, you and I are exceptions to the rule. Take me, now. Why should I retire?"

> *The New York Times, Report from Red China*

ON GETTING OLD

In spirit always young, but my material base is getting older and older.

> Interview, with William Attwood, Robert L. Keatley, and Seymour Topping, July 21, 1971. *The New York Times*, July 23, 1971

ABOUT THE POSITION OF THE OVERSEAS CHINESE

As regards the overseas Chinese in South Asian countries . . . we . . . urged upon them to respect the laws and customs of the country of their residence, work for closer friendship with the people among whom they have come to live and strive for still more cordial relations between China and the country in which they reside.

> "Report on Visit to Eleven Countries in Asia and Europe," March 5, 1957

ON INTERMARRIAGE AND FOREIGN LIVING FOR CHINESE

On this point the Chinese are rather conservative. Probably there are not many of Chinese descent who intermarried with your people [Canadians] . . . You know, in the olden days, overseas Chinese not only refused to intermarry with local people, but when one died, his coffin was brought back and buried in China.

But now it is not possible for them to send their coffins back, so they cannot but change their habits in this way.

And the second point is that they may stay abroad for many decades but yet not study the language of their country of residence.

Maybe this has changed amongst the younger generation. But as for the older generation, they just refuse to learn the language of their country of residence. . . .

I hope that these habits will be changed among the younger generation of those of Chinese descent living abroad. And I think maybe it has already changed. . . .

> Interview, with Canadian Trade Minister Jean-Luc Pépin, Canadian Broadcasting Company, July 2, 1971; excerpted, Toronto *Daily Star*, July 28, 1971

ON THE U.S.–SOVIET AGREEMENTS FOR STRATEGIC ARMS LIMITATION

The ink on the agreements was hardly dry before one announced an increase of billions of dollars for military expenditure and the other hastened to test new-type weapons, clamoring to seize nuclear arms superiority.

> *The New York Times,* July 18, 1972

II.

THE WORLD

CHOU EXPRESSES CHINA'S OPPOSITION TO FOREIGN INTERVENTION

Everyone knows that our people, after liberating our entire territory, need to restore and develop our industrial and agricultural production and our cultural and educational work in peaceful surroundings free from menace.

> "Political Report Delivered at the Third Session of the First National Committee of the People's Political Consultative Conference," October 23, 1951

Our socialist country will not be controlled by anyone.

> Interview, with Ross Terrill and E. Gough Whitlam, leader of the Australian Labor Party, July 5, 1971; Ross Terrill, *800,000,000, The Real China*

History has taught China important lessons, Mr. Chou said. "If we are only prepared for negotiations without preparing against armed war, that is not good," he said.

"If a war is launched against China, what should we do? How have we prepared? It may sound impossible to our friends, but we must think of it.

"Suppose the Soviet Army goes straight to the northern banks of the Yellow River, the Americans go to the southern banks of the Yangtze River, and Japan invades and occupies Tsingtao to Shanghai and India joins in and invades Tibet?

"What should we do? We are ready. We must dig underground tunnels, and this has been done in every big and small city.

"Only when one dares to engage in war, can one negotiate, and if one wants peaceful negotiations, he must be prepared against war. China has no soldiers abroad, no overflights of anyone's territory, and no naval forces on anyone's oceans or seas. We are holding on to our own territory and carrying out defensive measures."

> Interview, with some sixty Americans, including Huey P. Newton and John S. Service, October 5, 1971; *The New York Times*, October 7, 1971

The United States is a real tiger, and has shown its teeth. But if that tiger comes here, it will change into a paper one. Because the most powerful army in the world can do nothing against universal guerrilla action.

> André Malraux, *Anti-Memoirs*

In the first place we will not forget that any invading army becomes less strong than the people invaded, if that people is resolved to fight.

> André Malraux, *Anti-Memoirs*

When Western colonialism penetrated . . . into the East, this vast [Asiatic] continent, which in former times illuminated

Charlie Chaplin entertained Premier Chou En-lai at Chaplin's Geneva, Switzerland, home in 1954. *Pictorial Parade Inc.*

the ancient world with its wisdom, was plunged into suffering and disaster. . . . Our nations were humiliated and our people reduced to slavery. The independent development of our political life, of our economy, and of our culture was arrested and trampled upon, and the links between us, which date back for several millennia, were artificially broken. This common experience of suffering aroused in our peoples feelings of mutual sympathy. And these sentiments of sympathy have been further deepened by the struggles which we have carried on against a common enemy.

"Report on Visit to Eleven Countries in Asia and Europe," March 5, 1957; excerpt translated by Hélène Carrère d'Encausse and Stuart R. Schram, *Marxism and Asia*

What a pitiful position China occupied ten years ago in international affairs is well known. For many years, China had been a colonial and semi-colonial country. The imperialist powers regarded our country as rich booty from which everyone snatched what he could. The European imperialists tried to carve China up; the Japanese aggressors wanted to devour it alone and did swallow nearly half of it between 1937 and 1945. The United States, after the Second World War, was bent on taking over the place of the Japanese aggressors. China, the most populous country in the world, was not only deprived of the rights which were its due in international political life, but was almost deprived of the right to manage its own affairs.

The colonial and semi-colonial old China has now gone forever; the people's new China has emerged, independent and free.

Chou En-lai, *A Great Decade*

The Europeans have ceased to rule in Asia, and the Americans will follow them.

> André Malraux, *Anti-Memoirs*

The world could live in peace; if it doesn't, it is because of the misdeeds of the Americans, who are everywhere, and create conflicts everywhere. In Thailand, in Korea, in Taiwan, in Vietnam, in Pakistan—to name but a few—they are subsidizing or arming against us 1,700,000 men. They are becoming the policemen of the world. What for? Let them go home, and the world will have peace again. And for a start, let them observe the Geneva agreements. How can one negotiate with people who do not respect agreements?

> André Malraux, *Anti-Memoirs*

[Because the U.S. has so many bases around the world] the U.S.A. is now a man balancing an armful of eggs. He can't move or he will lose them all.

You can't catch fleas with your fingers. You can't lift a finger, don't you see, or a flea will get away. Such a man is fundamentally defenseless against all the untrapped fleas, who can choose where and when to mobilize and dine at leisure. [Chou clapped his hands together sharply.] That is the way to catch fleas.

> August 30, 1960. Edgar Snow, *Red China Today, The Other Side of the River*

MR. RESTON—Could I ask one final question about the U.N. and China? In your mind, is there a conflict between the basic principle of the U.N., namely, that all disputes between nations shall be resolved without the use of force or the threat of force, and the principle of revolution and support for national liberation movements in the world as espoused by your Government in the past? Is there a conflict between these two things?

MR. CHOU—No. Who has committed aggression against other countries? China hasn't. Over the twenty-two years of the history of our People's Republic, we only went abroad to assist Korea, but that was under certain conditions. We made it very clear to the so-called U.N. Command, composed of sixteen countries led by the U.S. We said to them that if they press toward the Yalu River, then we will not sit idly by, although at that time our Taiwan and Taiwan Strait area had already been occupied by the U.S. Seventh Fleet and the U.S. Air Force. It was the U.S. which first committed aggression against China, and not vice versa. It was only after the U.S. forces had reached the Yalu River that we sent our C.P.V. [Chinese People's Volunteers] to resist American aggression and aid Korea.

As for our help to other countries of the world, that is in the case when they are subjected to aggression. And in the view of the U.N. itself, aggression is wrong and should be stopped. So we are merely helping them to resist aggression. And in view of the U.N. itself, they should be given support. And a striking instance is Vietnam.

James Reston, "Transcript of Interview with Chou," August 5, 1971; *The New York Times, Report from Red China*

We are for withdrawing all foreign military bases from foreign territory. Of course this is a demand which can only be realized with the passage of time and with making efforts.

But China has served as an example in this field. We haven't had one soldier abroad and will absolutely not advocate sending troops abroad—in fact we're against it. . . .

Interview, with Canadian Trade Minister Jean-Luc Pépin, Canadian Broadcasting Company, July 2, 1971; excerpted, Toronto *Daily Star*, July 28, 1971

ON BEING A SUPERPOWER

Countries of the world, regardless of their size, should all be equal. We accept that China is a big country in terms of its huge population and also its size. Only the Soviet Union and you [Canada] are larger in territory. But our territory is larger than the United States. Our population is the largest in the world. . . .

But while we develop ourselves we will absolutely not become a superpower. . . . We will never be a superpower.

If our coming generations want to become a superpower then the Canadian press may criticize them—saying that you have violated the teaching of Mao Tse-tung. We are opposed to the power politics of the big powers.

Interview, with Canadian Trade Minister Jean-Luc Pépin, Canadian Broadcasting Company, July 2, 1971; excerpted, Toronto *Daily Star*, July 28, 1971

Our principles are clear-cut ones. We are opposed to the "major powers," to power politics and to domination. We will not become a major power under any circumstances. You are probably well aware of our position.

Interview, with Moto Goto, managing editor of *Asahi Shimbun*, Tokyo, October 28, 1971; *The New York Times*, November 9, 1971

If the statements of the small and medium-size countries are ignored and if things are decided only on the basis of statements by the major powers, this violates the premise that small, medium and major nations are uniformly equal.

Interview, with Moto Goto, managing editor of *Asahi Shimbun*, Tokyo, October 28, 1971; *The New York Times*, November 9, 1971

CHOU EXPLAINS THAT CHINA IS DEVELOPING NUCLEAR WEAPONS ONLY TO BREAK THE NUCLEAR MONOPOLY

Expansion of armaments, manufacture of nuclear weapons, and testing of such weapons of massive destructive power as nuclear bombs and guided missiles by individual states are of course detrimental to the cause of peace.

"Talk to a Delegation of American Youths," September 7, 1957

Should such a [nuclear] war break out, mankind would suffer a tremendous catastrophe. On this account, all the

Secretary-General Dag Hammarskjöld of the United Nations meeting with Premier Chou in Peking in 1955 where he sought the release of all U.N. Command Korean War prisoners, including 11 U.S. airmen who were sentenced to imprisonment on espionage charges by the Chinese People's Republic. *United Nations.*

countries of the world should have a share in the discussion of the question of complete prohibition and thorough destruction of nuclear weapons and the prevention of nuclear war.

"Talks at a Press Conference Held in Cairo," December 30, 1963

All countries will prohibit and destroy nuclear weapons completely, thoroughly, totally and resolutely. Concretely speaking, they will not use nuclear weapons, nor export, nor import, nor manufacture, nor test, nor stockpile them; and they will destroy all the existing nuclear weapons and their means of delivery in the world, and disband all the existing establishments for the research, testing and manufacture of nuclear weapons in the world.

"Letter to the Government Heads of All Countries of the World," August 2, 1963

No, we are not a nuclear power. We are only in the experimental stage. And what is more, that has been the case throughout the period from 1964 to the present, seven years already. We will not test when there is no need. We know it is quite expensive and a waste. And it is not beneficial to the improvement of the livelihood of the people.

It is quite clear, we can see, that the two big powers, the United States and the Soviet Union, have embarked on the mass production of nuclear weapons—cannot get down from the horse so to speak. But can they thereby monopolize nuclear weapons? No, they cannot.

We produced nuclear weapons by ourselves. We manufacture nuclear weapons because we are forced to do so in order to break the nuclear monopoly. And our aim is the complete prohibition and thorough destruction of nuclear weapons. And so every time we make a test, we declare that we will never be the first to use nuclear weapons. You will *see* what we Chinese say counts.

But we undertake not to be the first to use nuclear weapons. The people of the world have indeed noted the fact that these two big powers are using so much money on nuclear weapons. . . .

Since you do not want to have a nuclear war, then the United States and the Soviet Union should first undertake forthrightly that neither of them will be the first to use nuclear weapons, and then to go on to the next business. Because by reaching such an agreement, people will feel at ease.

> James Reston, "Transcript of Interview with Chou," August 5, 1971; *The New York Times, Report from Red China*

You may ask why does China want to produce nuclear weapons? We'll do that to break down the nuclear monopoly, to break down the nuclear blackmail. We have made it clear that we only carry out a limited number of nuclear tests when it is necessary. And every time we conduct nuclear tests, we conduct them at a time when the wind blows the radioactive dust first over our populated areas, before it goes to other countries.

What is more, we make it clear that the People's Republic of China will never be first to use nuclear weapons.

And every time we make nuclear tests, all the countries of the world, the heads of governments of all countries of the world, shall sit down at a conference to arrive at an agreement on the complete prohibition and thorough destruction of all our nuclear weapons. . . .

We believe the day will surely come when a prohibition on the use of nuclear weapons will be reached. And when that day comes you can export a lot of uranium to various parts of the world for the peaceful use of atomic energy. And in this way thermal energy will have greatly increased throughout the world.

We not only want to strive to have a peaceful environment for the good of our country, but in the world as a whole.

> Interview, with Canadian Trade Minister Jean-Luc Pépin, Canadian Broadcasting Company, July 21, 1971; excerpted, Toronto *Daily Star,* July 28, 1971

CHOU HAS CONSISTENTLY ADVOCATED BETTER RELATIONS BETWEEN THE CHINESE AND AMERICAN PEOPLES

The Chinese people are friendly with the American people. The Chinese people do not want to have a war with the United States.

> "Report on Asian-African Conference," delivered at the 15th enlarged session of the Standing Committee of the National People's Congress, May 13, 1955

There is no conflict of basic interest between the peoples of China and the United States, and friendship will eventually prevail.

> August 30, 1960. Edgar Snow, *Red China Today, The Other Side of the River*

In expanding its contacts with other countries, China proceeds from the desire to co-exist peacefully with all countries, including the United States, and not excluding any country. We are against placing our friendly relations with certain countries on the basis of excluding other countries. Even towards the United States we have the same desire for friendly relations. It is our view that outstanding disputes between China and the United States should not be an obstacle to friendly contacts between the Chinese and American peoples. Furthermore, we are deeply convinced that the day will come when the Chinese and American peoples, because of this traditional friendship, will resume their ties through their respective governments.

"On the Present International Situation, China's Foreign Policy, and the Liberation of Taiwan," delivered at the third session of the First National People's Congress, June 28, 1956

. . . the Chinese people and the Chinese Government desire to settle disputes between China and the United States through peaceful negotiations, and are opposed to the U.S. policy of aggression against China. But I would like first to cite one proof of this. After the liberation of China the U.S. Government declared that it would not interfere in the internal affairs of China, and that Taiwan was China's internal affair. Acheson said so in the White Paper and it was also admitted by Truman later. As a matter of fact, Taiwan was restored to the then government of China in 1945, after the Japanese surrender. It was taken over and administered by the then Governor of Taiwan, General Chen I, who was later killed by Chiang Kai-shek.

After war broke out in Korea in June 1950, Truman changed the policy and adopted a policy of aggression toward China. While sending troops to Korea the United States at the same time dispatched the Seventh Fleet to the Taiwan Straits and exercised military control over Taiwan. *Beginning from that time the United States started new aggression against China.** The Chinese government sternly condemned United States aggression in Taiwan and the Taiwan Straits. Shortly afterwards United States troops in Korea showed the intention of crossing the Thirty-eighth Parallel and pressing on toward the Yalu River [China's frontier], and, because of this, the Chinese Government could not but warn the United States Government that we would not stand idly by if United States troops crossed the Thirty-eighth Parallel and pressed on toward the Yalu River. This warning was conveyed to the United States through the Indian Ambassador. The United States Government disregarded this warning and United States troops did indeed cross the Thirty-eighth Parallel and press on toward the Yalu River.

The Chinese people could only take the action of volunteering support to Korea in its war of resistance against the United States. But this action *was not taken until four months after the United States stationed its forces in the Taiwan Straits and exercised military control over Taiwan,* and not until United States troops had crossed the Thirty-eighth Parallel and approached the Yalu River. . . .

After two years of negotiations an armistice was at last reached in Korea. *By 1958 Chinese troops had withdrawn completely from Korea.* But up till now United States troops are still hanging on in South Korea and will not withdraw. Moreover, the United States is still controlling Taiwan with its land, sea and air forces, and the United States navy and air forces are still active in the Taiwan Straits. . . .

---

* Italics express Premier Chou's original emphasis.

August 30, 1960. Edgar Snow, *Red China Today, The Other Side of the River*

Chou En-lai displaying the sword presented to him in the name of Hungary's Communist regime by Deputy-Premier Ernoe Geroe in 1959. *Keystone Press*.

China is a country which was blockaded by the United States for more than twenty years. Now since there is a desire to come and look at China, it's all right. And since there is a desire to talk, we are also ready to talk. Of course, it goes without saying that the positions of our two sides are different. And there are a lot of differences between our points of view. To achieve relaxation, there must be a common desire for it, so various questions must be studied, and all these questions may be placed on the table for discussion. We do not expect a settlement of all questions at one stroke. That is not possible. That would not be practicable. But by contacting each other, we may be able to find out from where we should start in solving these questions.

> James Reston, "Transcript of Interview with Chou," August 5, 1971; *The New York Times, Report from Red China*

The foremost thing, Miss Susan Shirk, is that the Chinese and American people wish to exchange visits with each other and this strong desire has broken through the barriers. So I recall what I said, that is what I said at the Bandung Conference in 1955. I said that the peoples of China and the United States *wish* to have contact with each other, friendly contact. It cannot be said that there was no response to my words. There were some, I believe a few progressive correspondents wished to come to China, but the Secretary of State at that time, John Foster Dulles, denied them that right. I believe that this issue could be found in the files of the State Department, and I don't think that they should be classified documents. (*Laughter.*) And in this way we were separated. But now we have passed through the sixties and entered the seventies. And it's your generation, your era, and you have broken through the barriers. And so with one sentence of

Chairman Mao's we invited the United States table-tennis team that wanted to come to visit China. And so they came! And the barriers were broken through. And so for this we must thank the new forces of your era. Isn't that so? And these new and friendly contacts are bound to continue. Because we received a very quick answer, and there was no way to stop the visit. And so now you also have come, and of course when you go back you will introduce new, even more American friends to us. Also some black friends. Of course if you would be able to introduce some minorities of the United States to us, we would be very thankful.

Let them all come to China to have a look. We will also return the visits, because your table-tennis team has also invited us to go to the United States, and our table-tennis team is also prepared to return the visit. Do you agree that the interpreter who works in the Foreign Ministry should go on the visit with the table-tennis team? (*Laughter and applause.*) Secondly, your CCAS, the Committee of Concerned Asian Scholars (*said in English*), has also invited us, and since you are so kind, I think that our young Chinese friends should also return the visit. There are a lot of young friends in Shanghai; they should take the lead.

> Interview, Committee of Concerned
> Asian Scholars Friendship Delega-
> tion to China, July 19, 1971

At the Bandung Conference I said that the Chinese people and the American people had always been friendly but the United States had occupied China's Taiwan and the Taiwan Straits and that we were willing to solve this problem with it through negotiations. The United States government agreed and the talks started . . . Finally Mr. Nixon himself knocked on the door, saying that he wished to come to Peking for talks. So well and good, we invited him for talks. Now the talks have not started but we are already in the U.N. This is a victory and we have not bartered away any principles.

Interview, with Neville Maxwell, the London *Sunday Times*, December 5, 1971

The development of the contact between people, in itself alone, is not enough because in the world of today, the state structures of various countries still exist. That is, different states still exist in the world today, and if there is no normalization or no restoration of the relations between the two states then it would be impossible for the contact between the two peoples to develop completely unhindered. And the governments of the two countries will bear the main responsibilities for the normalization of relations between the two countries and the restoration of these relations. If Susan Shirk was the president of the United States, then the matter would be easy to solve. But the problem isn't so simple. Isn't that so? But now, at the present date, in contacting your government to normalize relations we must contact those who are in authority in your country. But in your country, your system is that you have a president, and your president said that he wishes to move toward friendship and he also has said that he hopes to visit China. And of course, naturally we can invite him, in order to seek the normalization of relations between the two countries, and also to discuss questions concerning both sides. And this can promote the solution of the normalization and improvement of the relations between the two countries.

Interview, Committee of Concerned Asian Scholars Friendship Delegation to China, July 19, 1971

ON THE NEW TURN IN CHINESE–AMERICAN RELATIONS

The small ping-pong ball was served by Chairman Mao, and the way was opened.

Interview, with John McCook Roots, Thomas Manton, George Wald, et al., January 31, 1972

More and more [American visitors] have been coming. Though Japanese visitors have been the most numerous, the number of Americans coming should catch up with them in the 1970's.

Interview, with some sixty Americans, including Huey P. Newton and John S. Service, October 5, 1971; *The New York Times*, October 7, 1971

TOAST DELIVERED BY CHOU EN-LAI AT A BANQUET IN PEKING DURING PRESIDENT NIXON'S VISIT

Mr. President and Mrs. Nixon, ladies and gentlemen, comrades and friends. First of all, I have the pleasure on behalf of Chairman Mao Tse-tung and the Chinese Government to extend our welcome to Mr. President and Mrs. Nixon and to our other American guests.

I also wish to take this opportunity to extend on behalf of the Chinese people cordial greetings to the American people on the other side of the great ocean.

President Nixon's visit to our country at the invitation of the Chinese Government provides the leaders of the two countries with an opportunity of meeting in person to seek the normalization of relations between the two countries and also to exchange views on questions of concern to the two sides.

This is a positive move in conformity with the desire of the Chinese and American people and an event unprecedented in the history of relations between China and the United States.

The American people are a great people. The Chinese people are a great people. The peoples of our two countries have always been friendly to each other, but owing to reasons known to all, contacts between the two peoples were suspended for over twenty years.

Now, through the common efforts of China and the United States, the gates to friendly contact have finally been opened.

At the present time it has become a strong desire of the Chinese and American people to promote the normalization of relations between the two countries and work for the relaxation of tension.

The people and the people alone are the most motive force in the making of world history.

We are confident that the day will surely come when this common desire of our two peoples will be realized. The social systems of China and the United States are fundamentally different and there exists great differences between the Chinese Government and the United States Government.

However, these differences should not hinder China and the United States from establishing normal state relations on the basis of the five principles of mutual respect for sovereignty and territorial integrity, mutual non-aggression, non-interference in each other's internal affairs, equality and mutual benefits, and peaceful co-existence. Still less should they lead to war.

As early as 1955 the Chinese Government publicly stated that the Chinese people do not want to have a war with the United States and that the Chinese Government is willing to sit down and enter into negotiations with the United States Government. This is a policy which we have pursued consistently.

We have taken note of the fact that in his speech before setting out for China, President Nixon, on his part, said that what we must do is to find a way to see that we can have differences without being enemies in war.

We hope that through a frank exchange of views between our two sides, to gain a clearer notion of our differences and make efforts to find common grounds, a new start can be made in the relations between our two countries.

In conclusion I propose a toast to the health of President Nixon and Mrs. Nixon, to the health of our other American guests, to the health of all our friends and comrades present and to the friendships between the Chinese and American people.

The New York Times, February 22, 1972

TOAST DELIVERED BY CHOU EN-LAI AT A BANQUET IN PEKING DURING PRESIDENT NIXON'S VISIT

Mr. President and Mrs. Nixon, ladies and gentlemen, comrades and friends. First of all, on behalf of all my Chinese colleagues here, and in my own name, I would like to express my appreciation to Mr. President and Mrs. Nixon for inviting us to this banquet.

The President and his party are leaving Peking tomorrow to visit southern parts of China. In the past few days President Nixon met with Chairman Mao Tse-tung and our two sides held a number of further talks in which we exchanged views on the normalization of relations between China and the United States and on other questions of concern to the two sides.

There exist great differences of principle between our two sides. Through earnest and frank discussion, a clearer knowledge of each other's positions and stands has been gained. This has been beneficial to both sides.

The times are advancing and the world changes. We are deeply convinced that the strength of the people is powerful and that whatever zigzags and reverses there will be in the development of history, the general trend of the world is definitely toward light and not darkness.

It is the common desire of the Chinese and American peoples to enhance their mutual understanding and friendship and promote the normalization of relations between China and the United States. The Chinese Government and people will work unswervingly toward this goal.

I now propose a toast. To the great American people, to the great Chinese people, to the friendship of the Chinese and American peoples, to the health of President Nixon and Mrs. Nixon, and to the health of all the other American guests present.

The New York Times, February 26, 1972

THE TAIWAN KNOT

As for Taiwan, who occupied Taiwan? And so if you want to have a change, then you should act according to a Chinese saying, that is, it is for the doer to undo the knot.

James Reston, "Transcript of Interview with Chou," August 5, 1971; *The New York Times, Report from Red China*

The United States Government had insisted that the United States and Chiang Kai-shek have "the inherent right of individual and collective self-defense" in the Taiwan region. In other words, it would also legalize United States aggression in Taiwan and the Taiwan Straits, and create the objective reality of "two Chinas." This is opposed by the entire Chinese nation. Suppose someone occupied the Hawaiian Islands and dispatched a fleet to the waters between the mainland of the United States and the Hawaiian Islands, or supposing someone occupied Long Island and sent a fleet to the straits north of Long Island, how would the people of the United States feel in such a situation? You can thus imagine how the Chinese feel. Did not the people of the United States rise up against the Japanese after Pearl Harbor was attacked?

> August 30, 1960. Edgar Snow, *Red China Today, The Other Side of the River*

As for us, we do not like armed struggle and we do not provoke others. Not only have we not gone to Long Island, we have not gone to Honolulu. Even with the United States Navy in the Taiwan Strait, we are for negotiations.

> Interview, with some sixty Americans, including Huey P. Newton and John S. Service, October 5, 1971; *The New York Times*, October 7, 1971

"If Taiwan returns to the motherland, then its people would be making a contribution to the motherland for which we should give them a reward," [Mr. Chou] added. "Far from exacting revenge on them, we will reward them."

"How Taiwan will be liberated is our internal affair," he said, adding, "It will not be all that difficult."

"Chiang Kai-shek is opposed to the so-called two Chinas and is also opposed to one China and one independent entity of Taiwan," he continued. "In the past we have been allied with Chiang Kai-shek, and we became hostile to him, but on this question we have our common point. There can be only one China. So a way can be found."

"Once this problem is solved, then all other problems can be solved," Mr. Chou said. "The People's Republic would then be able to establish diplomatic relations with the United States."

Interview, with Canadian Trade Minister Jean-Luc Pépin, Canadian Broadcasting Company, July 2, 1971; excerpted, Toronto *Daily Star*, July 28, 1971

I would like to take this opportunity to reaffirm our stand: *the first point,* that is, if state relations are to be established with China, then it must be recognized that the government of the People's Republic of China is the sole legitimate government representing the Chinese people. *Second,* Taiwan is a province of China and it is an inalienable part of China's territory. And after the Second World War Taiwan had already been restored to China. And the liberation of Taiwan by the Chinese people is an internal affair of China which brooks no foreign intervention. *Third,* the so-called theory that the status of Taiwan is yet unsettled, which is the theory that is going about, some people in the world are spreading it, is absurd. That is, toward the end of the nineteenth century, in 1894, China was at war with Japan and China was defeated in that war, and after China's defeat, Taiwan was

President Julius Nyerere of Tanzania greets the Chinese Premier on his arrival at the Dar es Salaam airport. The Premier visited Tanzania for five days in 1965. *Keystone Press.*

taken away by Japan, *but* during the Second World War in the Cairo Declaration and later in the Potsdam Proclamation, it was reaffirmed that Taiwan should be returned to China. And then in 1945, when Japan surrendered, the Chinese government at the time had already accepted the return of Taiwan to China . . . in taking Taiwan back.

Fourth point. We oppose any advocation of a two-China policy, a one-China-one-Taiwan policy, or any similar policy. And if such a situation continues in the United Nations, we will not go there.

Fifth point. We are resolutely opposed to the so-called "Taiwan Independence Movement." Because the people in Taiwan are *Chinese.* Taiwan was originally a province of China. And a thousand years ago it had already become a part of China. The dialect spoken in Taiwan is the same dialect spoken in the area around Amoy in Fujian Province. Of course there are minority nationalities like the Kaoshan nationality in Taiwan, the minority that lives on the high hills. There is the same case on the mainland. There are also various national minorities on the mainland and we pursue a policy of national equality. Besides, the "Taiwan Independence Movement" is *not* a native movement in itself. It is a special movement which has behind it the special manipulation from foreign forces. One of their leaders is P'eng Ming-min who was originally a student at Harvard, who then went back to Taiwan to become a professor, and now is also back in the United States. There are also some elements of them in Japan. They are supported by the Japanese government.

The Sixth point. The United States should withdraw *all* of their military strength and military installations from Taiwan and the Taiwan Straits. And the defense treaty which was concluded between the United States and Chiang Kai-shek in 1954 about the so-called "defense of Taiwan and Penghu" is illegal, and null and void, and the Chinese people do not recognize that treaty. This is our stand. And we stick to our stand. And our stand has not changed from the beginning of the ambassadorial talks between China and the United States that began on the first of August, 1955, first in Geneva, and later on in Warsaw. They began after the Bandung Conference.

> Interview, Committee of Concerned Asian Scholars Friendship Delegation to China, July 19, 1971

Look at the outcome of the voting in the U.N. We did not expect it so quickly and it is possible that the United States, too, did not expect such a disastrous defeat for its "Two-China" formula. The result is that the door has been opened. People say since Nixon may go to China why can't we go too?

> Interview, with Neville Maxwell, the London *Sunday Times*, December 5, 1971

The activities and direction of United States policy toward China have been aimed at manufacturing "two Chinas." In this respect, both the Republican and the Democratic parties aim at the same thing . . . This scheme would probably be opposed not only by mainland China, but also by the Kuomintang in Taiwan and the Chinese in Taiwan. Therefore such an approach would lead nowhere, but in the solution of Sino-U.S. relations it would tie things up in knots.

> August 30, 1960. Edgar Snow, *Red China Today, The Other Side of the River*

ON AMERICAN INTERVENTION IN INDOCHINA

The facts are very clear. The Vietnamese people have not committed any aggression against the United States. It is the United States that has committed aggression against Vietnam. . . . In a word, the aggressors must withdraw from Vietnam and there can be no other alternative.

> Excerpts from a speech given in Peking, December 20, 1965

Although a third world war has not broken out, local wars have never stopped. I remember that your Secretary of State said that . . . about ninety small wars had been recorded. According to data of the United States, there were about sixty, and according to certain newspapers there were as many as three hundred. But it was the Indochinese peoples who paid the highest price in sacrifices.

> Interview, with Dara Jankovics of the Belgrade newspaper *Vjesnik*, August 28, 1971; *The New York Times*, October 21, 1971

WAS AMERICAN BOMBING OF NORTH VIETNAM AN EFFORT TO SAVE FACE?

Saving face? A brigand who has committed an armed robbery—can he save face by committing a second or a third? How many crimes are required before America's face is, as you put it, saved? In my view, the best way this bandit can save his face is by giving back the property he has stolen. The best way the Americans can save face is by withdrawing their forces from South Vietnam and by renouncing the right they claim to carry the war into the north.

K. S. Karol, "Chou En-lai Speaks," *New Statesman,* March 26, 1965

France, because of its defeat at Dien Bien Phu, did not wish to continue the war. It was willing to stop the war. But the U.S., which had begun to assist France—the Truman government of the U.S. which had begun to assist France in its aggression in Indochina—did not wish to end the war.

The British representative at that time was Mr. Eden, and he agreed to stop the war, but he wished to draw a line of demarcation and in this way to carve up, to divide the area and also to divide the world by drawing lines of demarcation. This idea of Mr. Eden's was suited to the needs of the brinkmanship policy of John Foster Dulles.

And although there was a clause in the Geneva Agreement that one day after the conclusion of the Geneva Agreement the representatives of the two sides of Vietnam, North and South Vietnam, should meet to form an election committee and that a referendum should be held under international supervision—although there was such a clause in the agreements, it was actually a false clause because they were not prepared to act upon it. Therefore, immediately following the Geneva Agreement, the Manila Conference was held at which SEATO was formed and a line of demarcation was drawn. Of course, SEATO has now broken up by itself, it's now gone bankrupt. But after the Geneva Agreement the election was not held and the U.S. assisted Ngo Dinh Diem to overthrow Bao Dai. The U.S. got control of South Vietnam that way. And all those who participated in the Geneva Conference are prepared to say, will admit, that if an

election had been held in Vietnam as stipulated by the Geneva Agreement it would be without question that President
Ho Chi Minh would have been elected in any case in Vietnam
because through the war of resistance against French aggression he had won great esteem, not only among the Vietnamese people but also among the people of the whole of
Indochina. But that was not able to come about and the
facts were the United States committed aggression, first in
Vietnam, which was then expanded to the whole of
Indochina.

> Interview, Committee of Concerned
> Asian Scholars Friendship Delega-
> tion to China, July 19, 1971

We think that the primary demand, a demand which must be
fulfilled before anything else, is a termination of the war in
Indochina and a withdrawal of all American troops and of
all their supporters from the outside, from that area.

I consider, therefore, that Indochina is the most acute
problem which must be solved. Of course, Korea is also a
very important problem, but a truce is in force there, whereas
in Indochina a war is under way. This is what the American
Government must understand if it wishes to bring about a
relaxation of tension in the Far East.

> Interview, with Dara Jankovics of
> the Belgrade newspaper *Vjesnik,*
> August 28, 1971; *The New York
> Times,* October 21, 1971

Such a small place as Indochina, with a small population.
Yet such a huge sum has been spent. The American Govern-

ment itself admitted that in ten years' time it spent $120 billion and suffered such heavy casualties. And the American people are unhappy about the American casualties. We on our side feel they are needless casualties. But the Vietnamese people have suffered even greater casualties.

James Reston, "Transcript of Interview with Chou," August 5, 1971; *The New York Times, Report from Red China*

CHOU COMPARES THE FRENCH EXPERIENCE IN ALGERIA WITH THAT OF THE U.S. IN INDOCHINA

France has learned the lessons of the colonial wars. She knows that they can't be won. That is why, each time I meet my French friends, I ask them: "Why can't you persuade your American allies to learn from your experience?" and each time I speak to my American friends I ask: "Why aren't you capable of producing a de Gaulle?"

K. S. Karol, "Chou En-lai Speaks," *New Statesman,* March 26, 1965

For instance, a complete withdrawal from Vietnam will be quite an honorable thing. What is there dishonorable about their withdrawal from Vietnam? I think that is most honorable. When General de Gaulle withdrew from Algeria, the whole world expressed their approval, and the Algerian people expressed approval, too. The relations between France and Algeria improved in de Gaulle's time.

James Reston, "Transcript of Interview with Chou," August 5, 1971; *The New York Times, Report from Red China*

This demand is even stronger than the demand to restore relations between the Chinese and American people. Because the people of the United States do not wish to sacrifice the lives of their people in a dirty war. Isn't that so? And therefore we believe that the question to be solved first should be the question of Indochina, and by doing so we would be satisfying not only the interests of the Indochinese people but also of the people of the U.S.

Interview, Committee of Concerned Asian Scholars Friendship Delegation to China, July 19, 1971

CHOU WARNS OF INCIPIENT DANGER FROM JAPAN

Japan has ambitious designs with regard to Taiwan. Japan wants to control Taiwan in her hands. So it's not a simple matter that Japan is supporting Taiwan in the United Nations.

James Reston, "Transcript of Interview with Chou," August 5, 1971; *The New York Times, Report from Red China*

We oppose the Japanese reactionaries. It is not that we have any hatred for the Japanese people. After the end of the Pacific war, we have not stopped our contacts with the Japanese people. New China has never imposed a blockade against them. The Japanese people have kept on visiting China, and we are also willing to go there.

The Japanese people are a diligent and brave people and a great nation. It was the U.S. Government which after the

The Premier in a 1966 photograph in a room at the People's Palace in Peking where he gives his press interviews. *Keystone Press.*

war strengthened the Japanese reactionaries. And when they have developed to the present stage they are bound to develop militarism.

Just look at the economic development of Japan. According to your President, the steel output of Japan is about to catch up to that of the U.S., as he said in Kansas City on July 6 [1971]. Why is it that Japan has developed so quickly? I've heard that you also admit that the reason was that not only was no indemnity exacted from Japan, but Japan was protected and provided with raw materials, markets, investments and technology.

And then there is another thing. That is, the U.S. has promoted the development of Japan toward militarism by the indefinite prolongation of the Japan-U.S. security treaty. The Japanese people are opposed to this treaty. And according to the report of the American congressmen who went to Japan to study the matter, Japan does not need such a huge defnse budget for its fourth defense plan for the purpose of self-defense.

The budget for the fourth defense plan reached the amount of more than $16 billion. And Defense Secretary Laird himself admits that according to Japan's present economic strength and industrial and technical ability, she will not need five years (1972–1976) to complete that plan, and two to two and a half years will be sufficient.

Despite this treaty, Japan with her present industrial capabilities is fully able to produce all the means of delivery, she is able to manufacture ground-to-air, ground-to-ground missiles. As for bombers, she is all the more capable of manufacturing them. The only thing lacking is the nuclear warhead.

Japan's output of nuclear power is increasing daily. The United States supply of enriched uranium to Japan is not enough for her requirement, and she is now importing enriched uranium from other countries. And so her nuclear weapons can be produced readily. She cannot be prevented from doing so merely by the treaty. You have helped her develop her economy to such a level. And she is bound to demand outward expansion.

Economic expansion is bound to bring about military expansion. And that cannot be restrained by a treaty. Look at all your nuclear bases in Japan. Even if you are to withdraw your nuclear weapons, the nuclear bases are still there, and they can make use of them.

When you said that there is no militarism, well, I'll argue with you on that score. This is not only borne out by the film which we have shown you and by the activities of Mishima [a distinguished general], who had committed suicide.

> James Reston, "Transcript of Interview with Chou," August 5, 1971; *The New York Times, Report from Red China*

When you oppose a danger, you should oppose it when it is only budding. Only then can you arouse public attention. Otherwise, if you are to wait until it has already developed into a power, it will be too strenuous.

> James Reston, "Transcript of Interview with Chou," August 5, 1971; *The New York Times, Report from Red China*

Just when you [Reston] were ill in Peking, you probably heard of the incident of a Japanese fighter colliding with a Boeing civil airliner, causing heavy casualties. Why? Because the air corridor in Japan is very narrow.

You have been to Japan. You know that the Japanese air corridors are divided into several levels, the higher for Boeings, the lower for the propeller-driven aircraft. And with the Japanese Air Force being equipped with more and more planes, they just fly everywhere with them at will for training. And the pilot of that fighter parachuted to safety but let his fighter collide with the Boeing. And when asked why they did that, the trainer just said that there was no place for training. What could they do?

That of course gave rise to public indignation. And among those voicing indignation were the opposition within the ruling Liberal-Democratic party itself, who said this is one of the harms of militarism. It is not something said by the Chinese alone; they themselves are saying that.

Of the four opposition parties in Japan, only the Japanese Communist party has differing views with China; that party supports [Premier] Sato on this question.

> James Reston, "Transcript of Interview with Chou," August 5, 1971; *The New York Times, Report from Red China*

The Japanese Socialist party admits to revival of Japanese militarism. The Komeito party admits that Japanese militarism is being revived, the Democratic Socialist party does not deny this fact, and the opposition wing of the Liberal-Democratic party also admits this fact.

> James Reston, "Transcript of Interview with Chou," August 5, 1971; *The New York Times, Report from Red China*

How was the Japanese economy developed? There is one characteristic of the development of their economy, that is, they made a fortune on wars fought by others, that is, the war of aggression against Korea and the war of aggression against Vietnam. Although Japan does not directly take part in these wars and Japan is a defeated power, Japan makes fortunes through these wars. For instance, the United States estimates that within the past ten years, $120 billion were spent on the Indochina War. And I believe that out of this Japan made quite a lot of money from the military repairs and transportation costs and costs for vacationing of the U.S. troops and also some means of communication. In all these fields I think Japan made quite a lot of money. And so twenty-five years after the Second World War, Japan, a defeated power, has now become the number two economic power in the Western countries.

Interview, Committee of Concerned Asian Scholars Friendship Delegation to China, July 19, 1971

MR. RESTON—You are really worried about Japan, aren't you?
MR. CHOU—Because you know we suffered a long time, for fifty years. Such calamities can be prevented by opposition from us and from the Japanese people together.

James Reston, "Transcript of Interview with Chou," August 5, 1971; *The New York Times, Report from Red China*

So there does exist this danger. But of course, the Japanese people of the present are not the Japanese people of the thirties or the forties, they have awakened to a certain extent. And also, what is more, the peoples of the Pacific and first of all the peoples of the Far East are no longer the peoples of the thirties or the forties; for instance, the people of the

Democratic Republic of Korea, the People's Republic of China, and the three Indochinese countries. And even those countries where there are now still stationed American troops, such as the Philippines, Thailand; or Australia, Indonesia, and also Malaysia, Singapore, they still have a fairly good memory of the disaster of the Second World War. I think the American people too remember the Pacific War. And first of all the Japanese people are aware of the fact that if Japanese militarism is revived, it will not be of benefit to Japan, it will be furthermore harmful to themselves.

> Interview, Committee of Concerned Asian Scholars Friendship Delegation to China, July 19, 1971

You too were victims of Japanese militarism. But you said the Americans are more forgetful. But I know you still recall the Pearl Harbor incident.

> James Reston, "Transcript of Interview with Chou," August 5, 1971; *The New York Times, Report from Red China*

KOREA—ANOTHER UNRESOLVED ASIAN PROBLEM

One of your generals [General Omar Bradley] admitted that the Korean war was a wrong war fought at a wrong time at a wrong place.

> James Reston, "Transcript of Interview with Chou," August 5, 1971; *The New York Times, Report from Red China*

And so now at the thirty-eighth parallel in Korea, there is a military armistice commission. . . . One side is the American representative and the representative of the South Korean puppets, and on the northern side there is a representative of the People's Army of the Democratic Republic of Korea and also a representative of China. They meet once about every two or three weeks. There's only a cease-fire, there's no other treaty whatsoever. According to international law the state of war has not yet ended and I believe that there must be people among you who study international law. It is the same case between China and Japan. The state of war has not been called off yet. We still have not concluded a peace treaty. And there are still American troops in South Korea. The Democratic Republic of Korea and we have both demanded that the United States should withdraw its troops from South Korea. Probably our friends at the Korean embassy have also talked about this. Because the Chinese people's volunteers withdrew from Korea in 1958.

Interview, Committee of Concerned Asian Scholars Friendship Delegation to China, July 19, 1971

CHOU EXPLAINS SINO–SOVIET DIFFERENCES

To have no difference whatsoever is impossible in the realm of thinking. Even in the thinking of a single person, one sometimes looks at a question in one way and at another time in another way. In a specified period of time, it is a natural thing that there are some differences between two parties on theoretical questions and on ways of looking at things. To be exactly identical would indeed be something strange and incomprehensible.

August 30, 1960. Edgar Snow, *Red China Today, The Other Side of the River*

The Soviet Union called off all their contracts with China in 1960. And particularly called off their agreement with us in the atomic field in 1969 in order to bring about a so-called spirit of Camp David.

But we make complaints to no one. We thank Khrushchev. Because by doing so he compelled us to rely on our own resources.

> Interview, with Canadian Trade Minister Jean-Luc Pepin, Canadian Broadcasting Company, July 2, 1971; excerpted, Toronto *Daily Star*, July 28, 1971

Many of our friends who come to China, they indeed feel that the way of life in the Soviet Union is not much different than that of the United States.

Of course, this may be going to a bit of extreme, but anyway. . . .

> Interview, with Canadian Trade Minister Jean-Luc Pépin, Canadian Broadcasting Company, July 2, 1971; excerpted, Toronto *Daily Star*, July 28, 1971

CHOU BEMOANS THE FAILURE OF THE 1954 GENEVA CONFERENCE

We don't want to be a mediator in any way. And we were very badly taken in during the first Geneva Conference.

> James Reston, "Transcript of Interview with Chou," August 5, 1971; *The New York Times, Report from Red China*

Lin Piao, who helped to compile *Quotations From Chairman Mao Tse-tung*, seen with Premier Chou En-lai in 1967 displaying their copies of the famous red book. *Pictorial Parade Inc.*

The question began in 1954. At that time during the Geneva Conference we reached an agreement. You friends who are studying various Asian issues probably have already read those documents.

And on this issue at that time we Chinese, and at the time also our Vietnamese friends, lacked experience in international subjects. At that time the representative of the United States was allowed to not sign the documents and to only make a statement that they would not disturb the agreement. But the reality was not so.

How could it be that a country which would not sign an agreement would agree to truly not disturb the agreement?

Don't you say that we were lacking in experience in such matters to allow this? You can criticize me for this. I myself, as one of the delegates on the Chinese side at that meeting, at that conference, accept your criticism.

Interview, Committee of Concerned Asian Scholars Friendship Delegation to China, July 19, 1971

The first stage of that [Geneva] Conference was devoted to Korea. I can try to describe the meeting to you. It was completely without results. On the final day of that stage, as there was no result whatsoever with regard to the Korean question, we put forward the question, what was the use of our coming. We said that at least we should adjourn, we should at least set a date for another meeting. At that time the foreign ministers of certain countries were persuaded, for instance Mr. Spaak of Belgium. He had worked with the United Nations. The chairman of the meeting at that time was Mr. Eden. At that time he wavered a bit and he tended to agree with this view. And at that time there was an authoritative representative who was seated at the conference and who waved his hand in opposition and the result was that it was not passed. You probably know who he was: the deputy of Mr. John Foster Dulles, Mr. Smith. Of course, it might not have been his own personal opinion but he did so on instructions. He didn't say anything, he couldn't find any words. He just waved his hand.

And as a result of this, the meeting was called off with no result whatsoever.

> Interview, Committee of Concerned Asian Scholars Friendship Delegation to China, July 19, 1971

THE TRICKY QUESTION OF THE BORDER WITH INDIA

It was with India that we had first reached an agreement on the five principles of peaceful coexistence. Because both China and India are two big countries, and in history there was no aggression by either against the other, with the sole exception of Genghis Khan's descendants who went to the subcontinent but then stayed here and intermarried with the local inhabitants.

As for the two peoples, we had lived together in friendship for generations. As for the boundary question, it was something left over by British imperialism. But precisely over this boundary question, they fell out with us.

> James Reston, "Transcript of Interview with Chou," August 5, 1971; The New York Times, Report from Red China

PREMIER CHOU CONSTANTLY AMAZES VISITORS WITH HIS DETAILED KNOWLEDGE OF CONDITIONS IN OTHER COUNTRIES—FOR EXAMPLE, CANADA . . .

Your GNP is more than $90 billion, but of course that included services. But if it were only for industry, agriculture, mining, transportation and communications, it would be only $60 billion or so?

And so for a country like yours with only more than 20 million population and a GNP of $60 billion, or maybe $90 billion with services—that would be quite a huge ratio compared with our ratio of the GNP to the total population.

Interview, with Canadian Trade Minister Jean-Luc Pépin, Canadian Broadcasting Company, July 2, 1971; excerpted, Toronto *Daily Star*, July 28, 1971

The question is how to really proceed on the path of independence, sovereignty and self-reliance. Of keeping a nation in your own hands. That is an arduous task.

I say that on the basis of perceiving your actual circumstances. From the situation which I have learned of your country, I know it is very natural for you to want to develop relations with various quarters . . . it is very natural.

Particularly your Prime Minister, His Excellency Mr. Trudeau, made a speech in Moscow in which he referred to this matter, and it was quite something for him to speak like that —because the situation in which he finds himself is different from the situation in which we find ourselves.

It is not an easy thing for a nation of 20 million to live side by side with a nation of 200 million. You need very strong will and patience.

Interview, with Canadian Trade Minister Jean-Luc Pépin, Canadian Broadcasting Company, July 2, 1971; excerpted, Toronto *Daily Star*, July 28, 1971

The people of the world all have such wisdom. For instance, the people of France and Germany are getting along much

A 1966 photograph of Chou En-lai gesticulating to a group of the
young Red Guards. *Keystone Press.*

better with each other now. They have been hostile with each other for about half a century.

So the people there will surely be able to get on well together. For instance, you can intermarry freely. Take for example what we cited earlier. The daughter of Mr. [Chester] Ronning married Mr. [Seymour] Topping [of *The New York Times*]. And they are on very good terms.

> Interview, with Canadian Trade Minister Jean-Luc Pépin, Canadian Broadcasting Company, July 2, 1971; excerpted, Toronto *Daily Star,* July 28, 1971

... OR LATIN AMERICA ...

Latin America is well worth studying, because that's your backyard. (*Laughter.*) That is to say, that your backyard is not always tranquil.

> Interview, Committee of Concerned Asian Scholars Friendship Delegation to China, July 19, 1971

[The superpowers have] carved up the various continental areas and now want to carve up the oceans. So the Latin American countries put forward the position that their territorial sea extends out a distance of two hundred nautical miles and that is indeed a great decision on their part— that's quite something. And according to this proposal, the Mediterranean would become the Mediterranean of the Mediterranean countries, and no other country can use the

Mediterranean as open seas. Of course, other countries may be allowed to pass through the Mediterranean. Friendly countries are still accepted. The point is that the Latin American countries put forth such demands because they are compelled to do so by circumstance or compelled to do so to protect their fisheries.

> Interview, Committee of Concerned Asian Scholars Friendship Delegation to China, July 19, 1971

... AND PORTUGUESE AFRICA

[On U.N. admission vote] Portugal voted for us also. Portugal has colonies in Africa but China supports the national liberation movement of the peoples in Angola, Mozambique and Guinea. Because of this, Portugal may be thinking as follows: We have supported China, so China should not attack us on the colonial question in the U.N. Security Council. This, however, is something we cannot agree to.

> Interview, with Moto Goto, managing editor of *Asahi Shimbun*, Tokyo, October 28, 1971; *The New York Times*, November 9, 1971

CHINA'S ADMISSION TO THE UNITED NATIONS

China has thus far been kept outside the United Nations. . . . She has not enjoyed her due position up till now, and other big powers are making attempts to ostracize her. What stand do we take? Our stand is to wait.

Speech at banquet given by Ethiopian Emperor Haile Selassie I, January 30, 1964

Although twenty-six years have already elapsed since the United Nations was established, the Chiang Kai-shek group, which was overthrown by the Chinese people, occupied the Chinese seat throughout. This is completely irrational and unendurable, and the phenomenon today is the result of an explosion of piled-up emotions. That the Albanian resolution was approved by more than a two-thirds majority— seventy-six votes for and thirty-five against—is irrefutable proof.

Interview, with Moto Goto, managing editor of *Asahi Shimbun*, Tokyo, October 28, 1971; *The New York Times*, November 9, 1971

In connection with our attitude toward the United Nations, there is an old Chinese saying which goes, "Be careful when facing a problem." We do not have too much knowledge about the United Nations and are not too conversant with the new situation which has arisen in the United Nations. We must be very cautious. This does not mean, however, that we do not have self-confidence; it means that caution is required and that we must not be indiscreet and haphazard.

Interview, with Moto Goto, managing editor of *Asahi Shimbun*, Tokyo, October 28, 1971; *The New York Times*, November 9, 1971

THE CHINESE STATESMAN CALLS FOR WORLD PEACE

The peoples of all the countries we visited strongly desire peace and abhor war. For centuries the Asian and African peoples have tasted enough of the bitterness of aggressive war. None of the Asian and African peoples that have just freed themselves from colonial oppression are willing to be dragged into war. On the contrary, only in a peaceful international environment can the Asian and African peoples build up their motherland, secure a stable and happy life. . . . Precisely for this reason, when thousands upon thousands of people came forward to greet us everywhere during our visits, the slogan "peace" was always the most conspicuous and resounding of all.

"Report on Visit to Eleven Countries in Asia and Europe," March 5, 1957

Exchange in the cultural field among the peoples of different countries, like cooperation in the economic field, is an important factor contributing to the consolidation of peace, friendship and cooperation among nations. Historically, the peoples of different countries have always enriched and advanced their cultures through learning from one another and drawing on each other's fine qualities.

"On the Present International Situation, China's Foreign Policy, and the Liberation of Taiwan," delivered at the third session of the First National People's Congress, June 28, 1956

We advocate peaceful coexistense and peaceful competition between countries having different social systems, and that the people of each country should choose their political and economic systems and their way of life for themselves. We are firmly opposed to the use of force or any other means to interfere in the internal affairs of another country and to prevent its people from making their own choice.

> "Political Report Delivered at the Second Session of the Second National Committee of the Chinese People's Political Consultative Conference," January 30, 1956

The general trend of the world situation is toward relaxation and progress. The forces for peace are constantly growing, while the forces of war are becoming more and more isolated. So long as the socialist countries, the nationalist countries, and all peace-loving countries and peoples unite and persist in their struggle, the Chinese people will take up their due responsibility and continue to make persistent efforts for the cause of world peace and human progress.

> "Report on Visit to Eleven Countries in Asia and Europe," March 5, 1957

It is indeed true that the world is undergoing changes. But these changes must not cause further damage to the Chinese people. Over the past twenty years and more, it's not we who have caused harm to others, but the U.S. Government who have been causing harm to other countries and other peoples. We have waited already for more than twenty years and we can wait for another year. That doesn't matter. But there must be a just solution.

> James Reston, "Transcript of Interview with Chou," August 5, 1971; The New York Times, Report from Red China

III.
CHINA

CHOU OUTLINES GOALS AND PROBLEMS IN BUILDING THE NEW CHINA

China is a poor country, but our first priority has been to feed our people, and that we have done.

> Interview, with a group of visiting Americans, including journalist John McCook Roots, *The New York Times,* February 6, 1972

China has no income tax, no unemployed and not a single soldier outside its own territory.

> Interview, with Dr. Arthur W. Galston and Dr. Ethan Signer, spring 1971. *The New York Times,* June 5, 1971

We are not now trying to get a rapid increase in cultivated acreage, although it is going on all the time. You can see that we want first to establish effective control over and efficient use of what land is already under the plow—more scientific agriculture in every respect.

> August 30, 1960. Edgar Snow, *Red China Today, The Other Side of the River*

Here we advocate family planning, but of course our increases in population are still too high. Our plan is to decrease the net population increase to about one percent in the seventies and if we can make it even lower than one percent in the eighties it would be even better. We're able to realize this goal of about one percent population increase per year in the big cities but it's still difficult to realize in the countryside. Japan is doing better in this field than we are. The population increase per year is about one percent. But, of course, it's the question of the livelihood of each individual family too. Our contraceptive pills are all free of charge as of last year.

> Interview, with Canadian Trade Minister Jean-Luc Pépin, Canadian Broadcasting Company, July 2, 1971; excerpted, Toronto *Daily Star*, July 28, 1971

CHOU TELLS EDGAR SNOW HOW DIFFICULT IT IS TO LIMIT POPULATION GROWTH IN CHINA. IN RESPONSE TO SNOW'S QUESTION ON STERILIZATION, HE REPLIES:

I'm afraid your question will give people the impression that I am a Marxist who advocates having no offspring. This would be absurd. . . . We do believe in planned parenthood, but it is not easy to introduce all at once in China, and it is more difficult to achieve in rural areas, where most of our people live, than in the cities.

The first thing is to encourage late marriages. The years twenty to thirty are very important to mental and physical development, during which scientific and artistic growth and talent often occur most rapidly.

Among various means of deferred parenthood or birth control, sterilization is practiced in many countries of the world, but heretofore mainly on women, not men. That not only imposes inequality on women but what is more, as I have been told by many doctors, sterilization is simple and harmless for men while more complicated for women.

In China, however, which has just freed itself from semifeudalism, there is great resistance among men to the practice of sterilization to curtail excessive reproduction. Others are likely to say that such a man has been castrated; he has become a eunuch!

Interview, with Edgar Snow, *The New York Times*, February 3, 1964

These sudden rains are common here. Once I was walking around this lake when I got caught in a storm. I took refuge in a nearby house. The housewife invited me to eat some stewed apricots—very delicious. It was a new house, clean and comfortable, and I learned she belonged to one of the families displaced by the dam. Her family had lived there for generations. She said many of the peasants had opposed being moved at first but now everybody was delighted with the change. No more fear of flood or drought, new and better land, electricity—and lake fish to eat! That was an interesting experience.

August 30, 1960. Edgar Snow, *Red China Today, The Other Side of the River*

If during the revolution we needed intellectuals, for the work of construction we needed them even more. Indeed, owing to the fact that before the liberation our country was culturally and scientifically backward, it was all the more important for us to make the best use of the intellectuals carried over from the old society in order that the intelligentsia might serve the socialist construction of our country.

"Report on the Question of Intellectuals," January 14, 1956

In some places, intellectuals are not employed or placed in accordance with their special knowledge and ability. There are scientists who want to do scientific research work, and who could thereby make their most useful contribution to the country, yet they are assigned to administrative posts in offices or schools. There are some experts who, because assigned to the wrong posts, are most unreasonably told to undertake tasks they have never studied. In some cases they are asked to do one thing one day and something quite different the next, but are not allowed to go back to their own fields . . . What a serious loss this is!

"Report on the Question of Intellectuals," January 14, 1956

In the past few years, since we were confronted with many different tasks at once, it was inevitable and quite understandable that we should devote more energy to projects immediately required and to technical matters, while paying comparatively less attention to long-term needs and theoretical work. But now if we continue to pay less attention to long-term needs and theoretical work, we shall be making a very grave mistake. Without a foundation of theoretical research in science, there can be no basic improvements or reforms in technique. However, the growth of theoretical strength is always a little slower than that of technical strength and the effects of theoretical work are usually indirect and

President Nixon and Premier Chou En-lai pose together on February 28, 1972, before Nixon's departure for the United States. In the center is Chang Ch'un-ch'iao, chairman of China's Revolutionary Committee. *Wide World Photos.*

not immediately apparent. . . . Of course, theory must not be divorced from practice and we must oppose the carrying on of theoretical research in isolation from practice. But the main tendency at present is the neglect of theoretical study.

"Report on the Question of Intellectuals," January 14, 1956

The reactionary view that an economically and culturally backward country cannot realize socialism has long been torn to pieces by Lenin and Comrade Mao Tse-tung.

Chou En-lai, *A Great Decade*

It is necessary to build socialism with greater, faster, better and more economical results. Is it possible to accomplish this complicated and difficult task? The imperialists and bourgeois elements said that it was impossible. They asserted that "greater and faster" could not go together with "better and more economical," as this would amount to "keeping a horse running while giving it no feed." The right opportunists within our ranks echoing them, also said that it was impossible. But we firmly replied that it was possible, because we place our reliance first and foremost on the creators of history—the mass of the people. This is a force which the imperialists and bourgeois elements as well as the right opportunists cannot understand at all or can only understand imperfectly. Our country has vast manpower; and man as laborer, inventor and user of the tools of production is the decisive factor in the social productive forces and the most precious "asset."

Chou En-lai, *A Great Decade*

THE PREMIER EXAMINES ISSUES OF POLITICAL STYLE

You can see the two screens here are empty. Do you know why? Because in the past we had red slogans, red background and gold slogans on them, with some quotations from Chairman Mao Tse-tung. And it was very irritating to the eye, and Chairman Mao did not like it. At the beginning of the Cultural Revolution, there was a necessity to do so. There was a necessity to make it possible for Chairman Mao Tse-tung's thought to be grasped by the broad masses of the people. And in this aspect the vice-chairman of the Central Committee of the Communist party of China, Comrade Lin Piao, has made a great contribution. He selected some of the best quotations of Chairman Mao and made them into a book of quotations. At that time Liu Shao-ch'i and Teng Hsiao-p'ing were opposed to the application of the study of Chairman Mao Tse-tung's thought. So at that time Comrade Lin Piao was the first to do so and to advocate the study of Chairman Mao Tse-tung's thought, and [advocate] the book of quotations among the PLA [People's Liberation Army]. And as the Great Cultural Revolution rose up, the broad masses, the millions of the students and the other sections of the people rose up to participate in the Cultural Revolution. And in the movement, the overwhelming majority of the masses were able to grasp some of the crucial points of Chairman Mao Tse-tung's thought in order to solve some of the problems at the time. But by now the Cultural Revolution has deepened; it is already five years since we began. We now call it the stage of struggle, criticism, and transformation, and the time has come for us to study in a deeper way Marxism-Leninism-Mao Tse-tung thought. And those who have had some education should very conscientiously study the works of Marx, Lenin, and Chairman Mao Tse-tung. And therefore these formalistic things should be cut down a little.

Interview, Committee of Concerned Asian Scholars Friendship Delegation to China, July 19, 1971

I heard that you were asking why people weren't wearing the colorful cloth produced in the textile mills. It is because it is the custom today to live simply and therefore people like to wear simple clothes, and also as a symbol of discipline. In order to provide a symbol of learning from the People's Liberation Army, people like to wear army uniforms. And the style of simplicity is also in opposition to bourgeois degradation.

> Interview, Committee of Concerned Asian Scholars Friendship Delegation to China, July 19, 1971

We must not imagine that just because we are Communists we have some heaven-sent ability to lead intellectuals in the work of cultural construction, and that it is impossible for us to make any mistakes. Such a view is extremely dangerous. And it is precisely such arrogance on the part of certain comrades in certain places that has damaged our party's work. Whatever problem we tackle, we must be honest. "When you know a thing, say so; and when you don't, admit it." We must on no account pretend to understand something of which we know nothing at all; but it is essential that we transform our ignorance into understanding.

> "Report on the Question of Intellectuals," January 14, 1956

In ideological struggle, we must remember, a man will only change his ideas when he himself is convinced that he is in the wrong. Crude methods will solve no ideological problems.

> "Report on the Question of Intellectuals," January 14, 1956

THE PROBLEM OF REMNANTS FROM CHINA'S TRADITIONAL PAST

Get rid of all old-fashioned and outdated institutions and working methods, rely on the people, realize a government that is truly of the people, by the people and for the people.

Address at the Political Consultative Conference in Chungking, 1946

COMPARING OLD TRADITIONS AND NEW WAYS

For instance in the old society, I wore a braid, a pigtail. But, of course, you can't see it on me now, nor can you find the old photographs. And also now in China in all the cities and in the great and overwhelming majority of the countryside you can't see that phenomenon anymore. But I cannot dare tell you there is not *one*. For instance, the old custom of the people of Tibet was to wear their hair in braids. But of course the serfs in Tibet have already been liberated, and the old serf system, the aristocratic system has been overthrown. The laboring people have come to power. But I can't say that there is not a single pigtail left as a manifestation of the old customs, because none of the three of us has been there to inspect on that fact as yet. So if you come on your next trip, or if other friends come to visit China and visit Tibet, and you find some person who is still wearing a pigtail, they can take a photograph of that and publish it to show that what I have said has not been entirely wrong. And another factor or phenomenon, that is there are a number of women whose feet were bound before. This is also a thing left over from the old society, the old system. For instance, my mother had her feet bound. Of course she passed away. So there are no people in Chinese society who have bound feet now? There still are. This seems a very new experience for foreign friends, for instance, our friends from the United States. For instance, if you want to take photographs of this, Chairman Mao has said you can take photographs of this. . . . But naturally because that's a phenomenon which the old society should be held responsible for. We are not responsible for that phenomenon. We were the ones who overthrew the old society, the old system. Of course now after Liberation we have been persuading people not to bind their feet, but what about the old people, their feet have already been bound, and you cannot cut off their feet, nor can they be restored to the original shape, because the bones were broken. There is no way to restore it. And if you did not bind the feet after they have been deformed to such a shape then the women would not be able to walk. And we cannot attempt to hide them all at home. If we attempted to do so, that would be a reactionary way of doing things. For instance, my mother had bound feet. But if it were not for her, how would I have come to be? And my mother herself cannot be responsible for having her feet bound either; she was also sacrificed by the old society. So when foreign friends take pictures of such things, for instance bound feet, you must investigate to see from what position, from what point of view they conceive of doing so. . . . The new society always grows up upon the basis of the old society. If there were not the old, where would the new come from? They are opposites, they are in opposition to each other. It's a dialectical matter. If this is a philosophical question, I will have to ask these two comrades [Yao Wen-yuan and Chang Ch'un-ch'iao, members of the Politburo]. Who are there among you who would like to talk about philosophy? Later on you can have your say. But I haven't finished yet. (Laughter.) The question arose from the taking of photographs. If you take photographs of this sort of comparison between the old and new society, that's one thing; for instance, when you went to Canton I believe you saw a people's commune. The women there do not have bound feet. Their feet are very large and they go barefoot into the rice fields. They are very healthy and strong, isn't that so? And if you take two photographs, one of each phenomenon, wouldn't that be a comparison between the old and the new society? (*To Dorothy Kehl.*) You're from Xinhui, you know that the women go barefoot and their feet are very large, and they carry things on their shoulders. That can serve as evidence. So Chairman Mao does not agree to not allowing people to take photographs. Since you're allowed to go to a place, why shouldn't people be allowed to take photographs of what they see? Therefore, if any of you want to take photographs today you are welcome to do it. Please do so.

Interview, Committee of Concerned Asian Scholars Friendship Delegation to China, July 19, 1971

Well, our great proletarian cultural revolution is now only in its later stages of what you call struggle, criticism and transformation. That is to say, to criticize and repudiate those old practices which are not beneficial to the people. For instance, various methods of teaching programs of the past which are not beneficial to the people, but this stage of transformation is only in the preliminary stages. . . . Because the education system remained the old system, and its methods the old methods, so education was divorced from socialism—divorced from production and was not in the interest of serving the proletariat, of linking itself up with production. And so when the graduates go to factories or to a farm, or to some government department, they must learn anew their specialty because their knowledge was confined to the knowledge of the books. They do not have any practical experience.

Interview, with Canadian Trade Minister Jean-Luc Pépin, Canadian Broadcasting Company, July 2, 1971; excerpted, Toronto *Daily Star*, July 28, 1971

It was a most difficult task to take over the government on the basis of the old society twenty-two years ago.

In fact, when Chiang Kai-shek was driven out, all the old things were left over by him on the mainland. He just took with him about one million—including some part of his troops, his officers, and his bureaucrats.

But . . . three million troops and officers . . . they were wiped out by us. Mind you, wiped out means some of them were killed in battle.

But the great majority of them were either taken prisoner or just scattered in society. And we must transform these people.

Some of them just went in the factories and countrysides to take part in productive labor.

As for members of the Kuomintang, Chiang Kai-shek's party, the great majority of them remain on the mainland. And so with these former officers and responsible members of the Kuomintang party—they just disappeared into society and turned themselves into ordinary workers, or office workers, or something like that.

And at the early years after Liberation, there were still shops and enterprises owned privately, by private merchants. As for those of the countryside, the landlords and rich peasants had land divided up among the peasants. But they still remained in the countryside, and they too were given a share of the land, and they remained in the countryside and some of them may have even joined the commune.

So if you add up the landlords, rich peasants, bourgeoisie, and also the bourgeois intellectuals, they amount to tens of millions, several tens of millions. In fact, including family members, over fifty million.

We couldn't send all these fifty million abroad. Whom would we give them to? You don't want them over there.

We couldn't wipe them all out. We're opposed to that. We're opposed to killing too many people. We won't do that.

Even the last emperor of the Ching Dynasty . . . was left in Peking, transformed by us. We looked after him until his death three years ago.

President Nixon followed by Premier Chou En-lai, center, a Hangchow official, and a Chinese interpreter stride across a bridge at Hangchow during President Nixon's visit to China in 1972. *Wide World Photos.*

And a lot of former Chiang Kai-shek high-ranking officers, including some generals—hundreds in fact—the overwhelming majority have been pardoned and are living well on the mainland.

But I just say this to show that the old remnants are to be found everywhere in China. So our socialist revolution is not a revolution which can be completed upon the declaration or formation of our government. Nor is it solved by changing the lease of ownership.

> Interview, with Canadian Trade Minister Jean-Luc Pépin, Canadian Broadcasting Company, July 2, 1971; excerpted, Toronto *Daily Star,* July 28, 1971

CHOU ALWAYS STRESSES THAT DESPITE MANY PROBLEMS, CHINA HAS TAKEN THE ALL-IMPORTANT FIRST STEP

China will never accept the return of Chiang Kai-shek. She has found freedom. It isn't America's freedom, that's all.

> André Malraux, *Anti-Memoirs*

Everybody knows too that ten years ago the political situation in China was abysmally dark and reactionary. The lackeys of the imperialists—the comprador capitalists, feudal landlords, warlords, bureaucrats, local despots and evil-minded gentry—rode roughshod over the people and bled them white. The broad mass of the people were in a state of slavery and utterly without rights. People of many national minorities suffered national oppression under the Han rulers in addition to oppression by the imperialists, and the aristocrats, landlords and slave-owners of their own nationalities. The country remained split for a long time; imperialist wars of aggression, the free-for-all fighting among different groups of warlords and the counter-revolutionary civil wars launched by the reactionary rulers continued for several decades and played havoc with the people. During the Kuomintang regime, bandits, gangsters, superstitious sects and secret societies ran riot everywhere; appalling lawlessness and utter disorder prevailed.

What tremendous changes have taken place in all this in the past ten years! The corrupt, iniquitous government which trampled upon the people is gone and has been replaced by an honest, industrious and hardworking government which really serves the people, a government of the kind the people dreamed of for generation after generation. The situation in which the people had no rights has ended once and for all; the broadest mass of the people enjoy democracy in law and in fact and to the widest extent in the administration of the public affairs of the country. National oppression has been eliminated; our motherland has become a big family in fraternal aid to one another. The country has achieved a unity of unprecedented firmness. Bandits, gangsters, superstitious sects and secret societies as well as prostitutes, beggars, gambling houses and narcotic drugs have all been swept away; there is law and order everywhere. The broad mass of the people, united as one and full of vigor, are building their own happy life eagerly, courageously and with boundless energy.

Chou En-lai, *A Great Decade*

You must add something to that. You must say that there has been progress made, but there is still a lot to work on. Otherwise the viewpoint would not be complete, would not be an overall view. . . .

There are also some phenomena which are in the process of moving from the lower to the higher stage. This is the way things develop. And also the standard of some things is being raised in the process of (consolidation?). If you only simply say that there has been progress, people won't believe you.

Interview, Committee of Concerned Asian Scholars Friendship Delegation to China, July 19, 1971

CHOU: For us, the darkest time in history was during our Long March, twenty-four years ago—especially when we crossed the great grasslands near Tibet. Our condition was desperate. We not only had nothing to eat, we had nothing to drink. Yet we survived and won victory.

SNOW: You must look upon your remaining national problems as by comparison easy to solve.

CHOU: Easy! Nothing about them is easy! Don't ever quote me as saying anything is easy here. Ten years ago, all China began a second Long March. We have taken the first step, that's all—the first step.

August 30, 1960. Edgar Snow, *Red China Today, The Other Side of the River*

IV.
THE UNITED STATES

GENTLE REMINDERS TO AMERICANS

The American sage Abraham Lincoln was right in saying that the country is of the people.

"Talks to the Delegation of American Youths," September 7, 1957

Talking about how the American Revolution was the first example of guerrilla warfare, Chou said: "George Washington started it."

James Reston, "Transcript of Interview with Chou," August 5, 1971; *The New York Times, Report from Red China*

Almost two hundred years now, isn't that so? Five more years before the two hundredth anniversary, to celebrate your two hundredth anniversary. Chairman Mao often likes to talk about when George Washington rose up to oppose the British colonial rule with only a population of three million. At that time England had probably a population of some tens of millions, twenty million or more—well, let's say maybe around ten times the population of the United States at that time. But you had the pioneering spirit, fearing no difficulties and the British colonial army was beaten by you everywhere. And the Americans at that time precisely carried out guerrilla warfare, firing from this corner and that corner. And you started your struggle in 1775. And afterward you elected George Washington to be your commander in chief—you spent your fourth of July in China. (*Laughter.*)

This is highly significant. And on your two hundredth anniversary you will come again. At that time you may only see two of us (i.e., *Chang and Yao*). At that time we will congratulate you. Five years is not a short time.

Interview, Committee of Concerned
Asian Scholars Friendship Delegation to China, July 19, 1971

CHOU'S INSIGHTS INTO AMERICAN FOREIGN POLICY AND THE INDUSTRIAL COMPLEX

Yes, indeed, your American friends should have broad perspective and have a broad range of knowledge because as you know the United States has extended itself everywhere in the world. (*Laughter.*) After the Second World War, it stretched its hands out everywhere in the world. As Chairman Mao said, they look into other people's affairs everywhere in the world. And as a result, they were merely putting nooses about their own necks. And there is a saying in China, that that is like trying to catch ten fleas with ten fingers. When you are trying to catch one flea, another one jumps out. And the result is that all of them escape. And at the most, you can only catch one flea by freeing one of your hands and letting go five fleas instead. That is the predicament that President Nixon is now facing. But it would be fairer to say that it is not only of his own making but also something created by the system itself. Because after the Second World War, monopoly capitalism developed to such a tremendous extent. And in some of these things, not only did your president not preconceive it, not even you could preconceive it. As for us, we could even less preconceive of these aspects. So it is well to read that statement of your president on July 6 in which President Nixon said that to have fallen from such a state of grandeur twenty-five years ago to the present state of affairs is something which he couldn't even have dreamed of in those days. And the opposite of that is that people like you are rising up and taking action. But that latter part, referred to by Comrade Yao Wenyuan, is something which he did not touch upon. Just citing a single figure would be quite surprising which is relevant to every single one of you. The internal debt in the United States now is approaching $400 billion. And the interest being paid this year alone is already $19 billion. And that is the amount of the annual budget prior to the Second World War during the Roosevelt regime, that is, about $20 billion. So how was that conceivable at that time?

That is, the American budget from 1940–41 was that figure only. That was $20 billion. But the amount of interest alone to be paid in one year's time from 1971 to 1972 is $19 billion. That is the change over a period of thirty years. A number of you are apparently not even as old as thirty. Who is the youngest? And you too are only twenty-six? And so I see these changes over the past thirty years. Were any of you here born in 1945? That was just at the conclusion of the Second World War. At that time U.S. imperialists appeared to be almighty. The world is changing, undergoing tremendous changes. But the American people, you, should not feel any discouragement. There is great hope for the American people. Because you have contacts with the people throughout the world, and that is a very fine opportunity as was already found out by our good friends. What place is there in the world which you have not gone to since the Second World War? You have gone to all places in the world . . .

Interview, Committee of Concerned Asian Scholars Friendship Delegation to China, July 19, 1971

THOUGHTS ON THE PEACE CORPS

Apparently after some members of your Peace Corps went to other countries, when they returned to the States they came to the conclusion that it was wrong.

... It would be better a friendship corps than a peace corps. Actually the Peace Corps in itself is a good, nice-sounding name but they have misused the name, so that it now has a bad connotation. Anyway, what one should not do is to act in place of the people of that region. No matter what the population of a country, when that country sends people to another country they should go there for the purpose of serving the people of that country and after their work is done they return to their country. They must not demand any special privilege. When they go to that other country, they should have the same living standard as the local people and if they commit offenses against the law they must be dealt with in accordance with the law of that country. Even if that country is backward, still you must be dealt with in accordance to the law of the country. And I go back to say that the best way is "to withdraw of your own accord." If they show that they do not welcome you, then you should speedily return home. And if you die there, do not ask for any special treatment, just have the corpse cremated. And not to set up a plaque in your honor. We are opposed to that. Even now some places do that for our deceased, but we are opposed to it. And when your work of service is done, then speedily return. Even so, it is still not an easy matter to gain the full confidence of the local people. This is a long-term process, isn't that so?

Interview, Committee of Concerned Asian Scholars Friendship Delegation to China, July 19, 1971

The U.S. benefited from both World Wars, and the U.S. losses were rather small.

James Reston, "Transcript of Interview with Chou," August 5, 1971; *The New York Times, Report from Red China*

The American military-industrial complex now is not limited to the East Coast and to the central part of the U.S. but has also spread to the West Coast and the southern part of the United States.

Interview, Committee of Concerned Asian Scholars Friendship Delegation to China, July 19, 1971

"America has its merits," [Chou] said. "It was composed of peoples of all nations and this gave it an advantage of the gradual accumulation of the wisdom of different countries. You are also a big country. We both have about the same amount of land and room for development."

"Of course," he continued, "you plead that your economic and political system is good, but let's not argue about that. You will not oppose progress, and if you are going to make progress, of course you must expect change."

"You will undoubtedly develop faster because of your industrialization."

James Reston, "Transcript of Interview with Chou," August 5, 1971; *The New York Times, Report from Red China*

THE PREMIER OFTEN TALKS WITH AMERICANS ABOUT THEIR RACE PROBLEM . . .

So I don't quite agree with your estimate that the American people are easily forgetful. Any nation is bound to summarize its own historical experience. Just yesterday I met a friend who had come from the U.S. some time ago, and he said that among the Americans there are now some changes toward the black people and that is a good thing. And it shows that many white people in the U.S. are becoming awakened to the fact that it is not right to continue the exploitation and oppression of the black left over from history. So isn't that a summary of historical experience? And it is very good.

> James Reston, "Transcript of Interview with Chou," August 5, 1971; *The New York Times, Report from Red China*

. . . AND AMERICAN CHINA HANDS

That is a fine thing, to learn Chinese in America!

> Interview, with Ross Terrill and E. Gough Whitlam, leader of the Australian Labor Party, July 5, 1971; Ross Terrill, *800,000,000, The Real China*

Wide World Photos.

As I see it, some points of view of the China hands are outdated. For example, Mr. Fairbank [Prof. John K. Fairbank of Harvard] is a very old friend of ours. He has been quite familiar with the situation in China. I was surprised by his position [that Taiwan should be independent].

But we have great hopes for our old friends. . . . We must talk and dispute. They will see for themselves and may come to our view. On the other hand, if their point of view is correct, then we on our side should obey the truth.

Interview, with a group of visiting Americans, including journalist John McCook Roots, *The New York Times*, February 1972

ON CHINESE SCHOLARS IN THE UNITED STATES

I must say some words of sympathy for them. That is that they happened to be oppressed in the fifties, during the McCarthy period, and this was a great harm for them.

Interview, Committee of Concerned Asian Scholars Friendship Delegation to China, July 19, 1971

CHOU'S INTEREST IN U.S. POLITICS ENCOMPASSES POLITICAL PARTIES AND PRESIDENTS . . .

It's a terrible thing to be President. He has to look after everything.

> Interview, with William Attwood, Robert L. Keatley, and Seymour Topping, July 21, 1971; *The New York Times*, July 23, 1971

I have read some of your articles, and you said in one of your articles that you felt that your President lacked courage. But of course, in deciding to come to China this time, it is something which even the opposition party say others dare not do. So on this point he has some courage. Mr. Mansfield [Senate majority leader] himself said that.

> James Reston, "Transcript of Interview with Chou," August 5, 1971; *The New York Times, Report from Red China*

. . . AS WELL AS "THE MOVEMENT" AND THE PEOPLE

There is only one President in the United States now, but there are a lot of young friends like you in the United States, that is in numbers, and also no matter whether in quantity or in quality you are in the majority.

> Interview, Committee of Concerned Asian Scholars Friendship Delegation to China, July 19, 1971

You can see the American youth are gradually raising their political consciousness. According to our experience, it is always intellectuals who start out, because it is easier for them to accept revolutionary theory, and revolutionary experience from books. But for the movement to succeed you must go among the workers, because in the United States the working class is the great majority of the people, and the peasantry is quite small. And so to do that, you must go into them deeply. We have only our experience, but we are not at all well acquainted with your situation.

Interview, Committee of Concerned Asian Scholars Friendship Delegation to China, July 19, 1971

And I believe that it was also Miss Susan Shirk who said that though the revolutionary movement in United States is developing, it cannot be said that it would be able to transform the entire system at the present date. For instance, the opinions in your family differ, don't they? So you can see it will take time to transform society. In recent years, Chairman Mao himself has paid attention to the American situation and he has also asked us all to note the fact that it can be said that the United States is now on the eve of a great storm. But the question of how this storm will be developed exactly is your task, not ours. We can only tell you about something of our hopes.

Interview, Committee of Concerned Asian Scholars Friendship Delegation to China, July 19, 1971

. . . China places high hopes on the American people. It is our belief that the future will be decided by an awakening among them. Their potential and prospects are boundless.

Interview, with a group of visiting Americans, including journalist John McCook Roots, *The New York Times,* February 6, 1972

SOURCES OF QUOTATIONS

Boston *Globe*, July 5, 1972.

Chou En-lai
Address at the Political Consultative Conference in Chungking, Chungking, 1946.

A Great Decade, Peking, Foreign Languages Press, 1959.

"Excerpts from a Speech Given in Peking, December 20, 1965," *Peking Review*, December 24, 1965.

"Letter to the Government Heads of All Countries of the World," August 2, 1963.

"On the Present International Situation, China's Foreign Policy, and the Liberation of Taiwan," *Hsin-hua pan-yüeh-k'an* (Hsin Hua Semi-Monthly), No. 14, 1956.

"Political Report Delivered at the Second Session of the Second National Committee of the People's Political Consultative Conference," *Jen-min jih-pao* (People's Daily), January 31, 1956.

"Political Report Delivered at the Third Session of the First National Committee of the People's Political Consultative Conference," October 23, 1951.

"Report on Asian-African Conference," *Hsin-hua pan-yüeh-k'an* (Hsin Hua Semi-Monthly), No. 6, 1955.

"Report on the Question of Intellectuals," Peking, Foreign Languages Press, 1956.

"Report on Visit to Eleven Countries in Asia and Europe," *Hsin-hua pan-yüeh-k'an* (Hsin Hua Semi-Monthtly), No. 7, 1957.

Speech at a banquet given by Ethiopian Emperor Haile Selassie I, January 30, 1964.

"Talks at a Press Conference Held in Cairo," December 30, 1963.

"Talk to a Delegation of American Youths," *Chung-kuo chi'ing-nien* (Chinese Youth), No. 20, 1957.

Committee of Concerned Asian Scholars, The, *China! Inside the People's Republic,* New York, Bantam Books, 1972.

d' Encausse, Hélène Carrère, and Schram, Stuart R., *Marxism and Asia,* London, The Penguin Press, 1969.

Karol, K. S., "Chou En-lai Speaks," *New Statesman,* March 26, 1965.

Liu Ning, *The Autobiography of a Proletarian,* Chungking, 1946.

London *Sunday Times,* December 5, 1971.

Malraux, André, *Anti-Memoirs,* trans. Terrence Kilmartin, New York, Holt, Rinehart & Winston, 1968.

Newsweek, March 6, 1972.

New York Times, The
    April 15, 1971
    February 22, 1972
    February 26, 1972
    February 28, 1972
    July 18, 1972
    Attwood, William; Keatley, Robert L.; and Topping, Seymour, July 23, 1971.
    Galston, Dr. Arthur W., June 5, 1971.
    Goto, Moto, November 9, 1971.
    Jankovics, Dara, October 21, 1971.
    Newton, Huey P., and Service, John S., October 7, 1971.
    Roots, John McCook, February 6, 1972.
    Snow, Edgar, February 3, 1964.

Report from Red China, compiled by *The New York Times,* New York, Avon Books, 1972.

Roots, John McCook; Manton, Thomas; Wald, George; et al., January 31, 1972. Special cable from Hong Kong.

Snow, Edgar, *Red China Today, The Other Side of the River,* New York, Vintage Books, 1971.

Terrill, Ross, *800,000,000, The Real China,* Atlantic Monthly Press Book; Boston, Little, Brown, 1971.

Toronto *Daily Star,* July 28, 1971.